Cambridge Elements ≡

Elements in Shakespeare and Pedagogy
edited by
Liam E. Semler
The University of Sydney
Gillian Woods
Birkbeck College, University of London

DISAVOWING AUTHORITY IN THE SHAKESPEARE CLASSROOM

Huw Griffiths
The University of Sydney

CAMBRIDGE
UNIVERSITY PRESS

CAMBRIDGE
UNIVERSITY PRESS

Shaftesbury Road, Cambridge CB2 8EA, United Kingdom

One Liberty Plaza, 20th Floor, New York, NY 10006, USA

477 Williamstown Road, Port Melbourne, VIC 3207, Australia

314–321, 3rd Floor, Plot 3, Splendor Forum, Jasola District Centre, New Delhi – 110025, India

103 Penang Road, #05–06/07, Visioncrest Commercial, Singapore 238467

Cambridge University Press is part of Cambridge University Press & Assessment, a department of the University of Cambridge.

We share the University's mission to contribute to society through the pursuit of education, learning and research at the highest international levels of excellence.

www.cambridge.org
Information on this title: www.cambridge.org/9781108948692

DOI: 10.1017/9781108953115

First published 2024

A catalogue record for this publication is available from the British Library.

ISBN 978-1-108-94869-2 Paperback
ISSN 2632-816X (online)
ISSN 2632-8151 (print)

Disavowing Authority
in the Shakespeare Classroom

Elements in Shakespeare and Pedagogy

DOI: 10.1017/9781108953115
First published online: April 2024

Huw Griffiths

The University of Sydney

Author for correspondence: Huw Griffiths, huw.griffiths@sydney.edu.au

ABSTRACT: Based on real experiences of teaching Shakespeare in diverse classrooms and outreach programmes, this Element questions the role of authority in Shakespeare teaching. It connects an understanding of how Shakespearean texts function with critical thinking about teaching, especially derived from the work of Jacques Rancière. Certain elements of the Shakespearean text – notably how it was intended to teach its first readers, the actors, and its uses of dramatic irony – are revealed as already containing possibilities for more de-centred forms of knowledge production.

KEYWORDS: Shakespeare, pedagogy, Rancière, inclusion, authority

ISBNs: 9781108948692 (PB), 9781108953115 (OC)
ISSNs: 2632-816X (online), 2632-8151 (print)

Contents

Preface: On the T3 Train Line

This Element considers one way in which the question – or problem – of 'authority' might be reevaluated in the Shakespeare classroom. I will hold off on a description of 'authority' for a moment; hopefully, it is something that will emerge as I describe the teaching itself in the Element's several sections. For now, I want it to include the 'authority' of the teacher, but also of the institution of the university or school, and perhaps of Shakespeare himself. My impetus for writing this Element comes from an opportunity that arose thirteen years ago, when I was starting in a new job as a lecturer at the University of Sydney in Australia, specialising in Shakespeare. The Australian government at that time was pursuing a programme of widening participation in higher education, an aim that has been set aside by subsequent governments.[1] Back in 2008, funding was made available for projects that connected universities with constituencies that were underrepresented in their traditional student cohorts, all part of an attempt to both extend and broaden participation in higher education.

---

[1] This activity was predicated on the Bradley Review of Higher Education, a study commissioned by the Labor government of Kevin Rudd in 2008 and presided over by Denise Bradley, previously vice chancellor of the University of South Australia. One recommendation of the review was that greater participation in higher education be promoted by the government, and that a greater diversity of young people be afforded the opportunity to attend university. At the time of the report, around 14 per cent of the university cohort across Australia came from low socio-economic backgrounds, a figure which had remained steady for decades. The adopted recommendation was a target of 20 per cent undergraduate students to come from low socio-economic backgrounds by 2020 (Australian Government, *Review of Higher Education Final Report* (December 2008), p.ix). In 2022, the education minister for a new Labor government, Jason Clare, announced a plan to provide 20,000 new places at Australian universities for students from 'underrepresented backgrounds', including 'people from low socio-economic backgrounds, rural and remote areas, First Nations people, first in family and people with disability' (Jim Chalmers and Jason Clare, '20,000 New University Places to Target Skills Shortages', media release (17 August 2022)).

For the University of Sydney this undertaking presented a particular challenge.[2] It is the oldest university in the country with a reputation as a privileged institution that has, for most of its 172 years, catered for a middle class, mostly privately educated white urban elite. In the English department, a group of colleagues sought, through a successful application for some of this government funding, to broker connections with schools in two areas: suburbs in the west of Sydney that are characterised in official documentation as being low socio-economic status areas, and rural areas which, in Australia, can be a 13-hour drive or a 2.5-hour flight away from access to higher education. My colleagues who set up this programme invited me along to the opening stages of the project in case Shakespeare proved to be a point of connection and also because of my own background as a state school student (albeit in the UK) who did attend an elite university.[3]

---

[2] Across all universities in Australia, the 20 per cent target set as a low socio-economic proportion of the undergraduate cohort was not met, in part because their overall goal of increased participation was broadly successful with the new students not all coming from backgrounds identified as being of low socio-economic status (SES). At the University of Sydney, however, the figures are worse. Starting from a low percentage of 5 per cent, there is now just 7 per cent of the undergraduate cohort at the University of Sydney who come from a low socio-economic background. There is a lot of work to do. I am grateful to my University of Sydney colleague, Professor Tim Payne (Director of Higher Education Policy and Projects in the vice chancellor's office), for providing me with a guide to these figures. I can only hope that my own training in the idiosyncratic and anecdotal methodologies of literary studies is not showing too much in my handling of numerical data.

[3] The project leader from the start has been my colleague, Melissa Hardie, with administrative and research assistance provided by Kieryn McKay. The activities supported and developed by them, and by the project as a whole, are too numerous to mention but have included individual and group support for thousands of students across more than a decade. In recent years, the funding has been taken over by the charitable organisation, the Nelson Meers Foundation. Some flavour of this can be seen on the project's current website: www.sydney .edu.au/arts/industry-and-community/high-school-engagement/link-project-widening-participation-in-english.html.

The guiding note that we gave ourselves was to avoid any real or perceived paternalism, and to guard against undermining the schoolteachers' own considerable expertise in knowing how best to guide their students through the arcane world of Australian high school qualifications. Even though the project operated under an ethos of 'widening participation' in higher education, it was not something that we saw as a recruitment exercise specifically to the University of Sydney. For me, the most striking impression to emerge from initial conversations with teachers from the schools was the strong sense of physical distance between our city-centre university campus and the towns or suburbs that we were visiting. The distance between the university and schools in rural or regional areas of the state was obviously important but I was more fascinated by the *idea* of distance that held the university apart from the schools that we visited in the western suburbs of Sydney. Some of these schools are a little more than about thirty minutes train ride away from the university, along the same busy T3 commuting suburban train route that I regularly use myself. But, as we learned from the teachers who we met, the city centre (where the university is located) was somewhere that many of their students would hardly, if ever, visit. The T3 train line is a journey through the cultural as well as socio-economic variety of Sydney, starting in outlying towns and moving through outer suburbs, inhabited by characteristically multicultural and working-class communities before arriving in the inner city suburbs in which the university is situated, suburbs now mostly gentrified and inhabited by wealthy, urban, and mobile professionals. The T3 train line, of course, connects these parts of the city to each other. But it is also a mobile image of the multiply distinct communities that comprise contemporary Sydney, a city founded on settler dispossession of its indigenous populations and subsequently populated by migrant communities from around the world. For all of their claims to a kind of classlessness, Sydney and Australia as a whole are multiply stratified societies, formed as much through racial, class-driven, religious, and cultural conflict as by a shared space. To 'widen participation' in an institution such as the University of Sydney, a foundational institution of colonial power, is not a neutral activity.

Once the project was up and running, we decided to invite a number of different school groups on to campus for a day. One of the contexts for the visit became this sense of unfamiliarity that students had with the place that they were visiting, a sense of unfamiliarity with, in part at least, their own city. The potential for viewing the University of Sydney as an unwelcoming space is, no doubt, exacerbated by its nineteenth-century buildings, dominated by a slightly kitsch late Victorian neogothic version of an Oxbridge quadrangle set up on a hill, below which stretches the commercial centre of the city itself. The imperial architecture of the buildings would be equally at home in London, Edinburgh, or Mumbai. The campus is potentially impressive, as exhilarating as it is oppressive, but to feel that you belong amongst its buildings demands – and also breeds – a sense of entitlement; there is nothing about the original buildings that does not exude authority, privilege, and distance. As for the rest of the campus, the landscaping is beautiful, but its more modern buildings have become, through the twentieth and twenty-first centuries, steadily more alienating. There was a moment in the early to mid twentieth century when some human-sized buildings were built, first in arts and crafts style and later in some modernist structures such as the elegant and user-friendly Fisher library, constructed in 1962. But these are now sandwiched between earlier imperial gothic revival and more recent corporate architecture, equipped with all the features of contemporary commerce: ostentatiously oversized lobbies policed by intimidating and outsourced security staff. The walls are now more likely to be made of gleamingly transparent glass than gargoyled sandstone. But if you get too near, you will see that without the proper swipe card access will be denied. I describe this at length for two reasons. First, I want to capture a sense that the project made me look at the campus with fresh eyes. But, also, as we moved into the project, it seemed to me that the spaces of the campus loomed large in the conversations and questions of visiting students, as a means to articulate something about the cultural clashes underlying our activities. Where our usual cohorts of students often refer to the campus as 'Hogwart's', this was largely absent from the descriptions of visiting students. Fantasies of British mid century boarding school, re-imagined as either a school for wizards or a university for wealthy Sydneysiders, were not being entertained in these particular visits.

When it was decided to include Shakespeare as our main teaching activity for the first major campus visit within the project, I had to think hard about several things: how to construct an activity that would allow different cohorts at different stages of their high school English curricula to work together; how to make it evident to teachers and students what collectively we might stand to gain from the activity; how to ensure that the activity was authentically derived from the Shakespearean material; and, importantly, how to make people feel like they belonged on the university campus. How could I invite the visiting students to feel at home, to make the spaces of the university meaningful for them, at least for an afternoon? Teaching Shakespeare amidst the spectres of privilege past, present, and future is not an ideal way to start with any of this. And, yet, because of the centrality of Shakespeare to high school literature curricula and his prominent place in our own offerings, to ignore this connection would also be doing the potential relationship a disservice. Even as I write that last sentence, I am not so sure that it is true. I do think it important that an institution like the University of Sydney listen and provide the kinds of services that our surrounding communities want or need. And, in this case, it might well be providing high school teachers with an additional resource in their teaching of Shakespeare. However, this replication of Shakespeare as source of cultural capital that can be loaned out from elite institutions is also potentially very damaging. Doug Eskew puts this extraordinarily well in a chapter on teaching Shakespeare in Colorado State University. In conventionally 'bardolatrous' Shakespeare teaching – teaching that I would see as assuming Shakespeare's cultural capital as an automatic good – what might be produced is further 'alienation' in students:

> In places where bardolatry is still taught, a kind of ideological violence is visited upon the students. They are taught that Shakespeare speaks to the human soul at the same time that Shakespeare's transcendent words make no sense to them. For students in this position, to believe that Shakespeare speaks to the human soul is to acknowledge that either they are not human or they do not have a soul.[4]

---

[4] Doug Eskew, 'Shakespeare, Alienation, and the Working-Class Student', in Sharon O'Dair and Timothy Francisco (Eds.), *Shakespeare and the 99%: Literary Studies, the Profession, and the Production of Inequity* (London: Palgrave, 2019), 44.

The challenge, then, was not to fetishise the experience of 'doing Shakespeare' at an elite university whilst, at the same time, modelling a way of learning with the texts that might generate some agency on the part of the students themselves.

Much of the material of this Element emerges from the solution that I came up with in response to this challenge. It was a solution that focused determinedly on the act of *reading* play scripts but that also attempted to disavow my (or the university's) own authority in that act. I'll explain it as I go through the Element. That first day – the first of many – went fine and we all seemed to have a good time. I am even sure that we all (students, teachers, and university colleagues) learned something from doing the exercise that we set up. The person who I can confidently claim did learn something was me and, in writing this Element, I want not only to describe these activities but also to advance my own thinking about the impact of it all on my teaching. How might these solutions to a very particular set of teaching contexts inform a still-ongoing shift in my approach to the question of what it means to teach Shakespeare?

To do this I want, first, to move from one neogothic fantasy of dubious and fading authority (the University of Sydney) to another: Shakespeare's play, *Richard II*.

Introduction: 'Down, down, I come'

King Richard appears on the ramparts of Flint Castle; his opponents occupy the ground below. Richard has lost the war against Bolingbroke's rebels and it is inevitable that he will be forced to hand over the crown. Although everybody knows that his grasp of the English crown has fatally slipped, one of his enemies – the Duke of York – nevertheless describes his arrival as one that still befits his rank: 'Yet looks he like a king' (*Richard II*, 3.3.67).[5]

---

[5] References to Shakespeare's plays are taken from the New Oxford Shakespeare: William Shakespeare, *The New Oxford Shakespeare*, Eds. Terri Bourus, Gabriel Egan, John Jowett, and Gary Taylor (Oxford: Oxford University Press, 2016). References will be given in parentheses.

If we imagine ourselves in the audience watching this scene unfold in a performance of Shakespeare's play – a performance on a stage rather than on a screen – then the rest of York's speech directs us to interpret the appearance of the soon-to-be-deposed king in a very particular way. 'Behold his eye', York commands, addressing both the audience on stage (his fellow rebels, including Bolingbroke, the future King Henry IV) and the audience offstage (us). In the audience, we would be at some remove from the eye in question and so, unless we were very close and had extraordinary eyesight, we would not be able to follow the instruction to 'behold' it exactly. York, however, provides the details of what we *would* see if we could only get close enough to the lonely monarch: 'Behold his eye / As bright as any eagle's, lightens forth / Controlling majesty' (3.3.67–69). York tells us that what we are seeing is an eye that shines so extraordinarily brightly that it shoots out beams of light – it 'lightens forth' – and that those beams are both source and location of an imperious sovereignty, one that is defined and determined by the presence of the king's body, even as that body is re-imagined metaphorically as eagle-like. 'Majesty' is an important word in relation to kingship in the sixteenth century, one that implies the location of inalienable sovereignty in the person of a monarch.[6] With those beams of light, Richard is controlling us, or so we are told by a rebel who is about to assist in deposing him. It is a powerful description, and one that builds on Bolingbroke's own sense of awe at what is happening and at what he is doing by removing Richard from the throne:

> Methinks King Richard and myself should meet
> With no less terror than the elements
> Of fire and water when their thund'ring shock
> At meeting tears the cloudy cheeks of heaven.

> (3.3.53–56)

---

[6] The most influential description of sovereign majesty comes from the work of Jean Bodin, writing, 'As for the title "majesty", it is clear enough that it belongs only to someone who is sovereign' (Jean Bodin, *On Sovereignty: Four Chapters from the Six Books of the Commonwealth*, Ed. Julian H. Franklin (Cambridge: Cambridge University Press, 1997), 86).

Like the consummate politician that he is, Bolingbroke elides his own agency in bringing the situation about, focusing on the impressive but flawed majesty that surrounds the figure of Richard, and deflecting his personal responsibility into an ironic reflection on the underwhelming bathos of the event. In the twentieth and twenty-first centuries, we have learned a name for this sort of thing: 'gaslighting'.

If Bolingbroke's speech admits of a disjunction between what should be happening and what is actually happening ('Methinks King Richard and myself *should* meet / With no less terror'), then York's description seems much more like an attempt to control what it is that can be seen, producing the scene for us as his audience. Without York's words, what would we really be able to see? If we were amongst the play's first ever audiences, we would see the actor playing Richard walk on to a balcony in either James Burbage's Theatre or in the home of Sir Edward Hoby (two likely locations for *Richard II*'s first performances), presumably in a wonderful costume but surely not emitting laser-like beams of sovereign power.[7] York's words transform what we would see in any performance into something else, into something that is not physically there. More than this, his words produce the spectacle as meaningful. Inside Richard's eye, invisible to us, reside the central questions of this brilliant (intricate, smart, terrifying) play: what is sovereignty? Can sovereignty be disowned and removed, or does it always remain, at its origins, immutable? How do we know that at this precise moment of the play? How do we know that this is what the spectacle means? We know because York explains to us that this is what it means. '*Yet* looks he like a king.' He *still* looks like a king; despite what we think or do, he will always *be* the king. All of those implications can – so York tells us – readily be seen in that (imaginary) light-emitting eye.

---

[7] The Theatre was the playhouse used by the Lord Chamberlain's Men until 1596, one year after *Richard II* had made its stage debut. A possible first record of the play's performance is contained in a letter from Sir Edward Hoby, courtier and scholar, to Sir Robert Cecil, his cousin and the future Chancellor, inviting him to a performance of 'K. Richard' in December 1595. (Charles R. Forker, 'Introduction', in William Shakespeare (Ed.), *King Richard II* (London: Arden Shakespeare, 2002), 114).

When Richard responds to Bolingbroke and York, he goads his opponents – knowing that they know that we all think we know that he probably should still be king but that soon he won't be. Eventually, he is persuaded to descend to the lower level, to the 'base court' where he begins negotiations with Bolingbroke, negotiations that can only ever result in his abdication:

> Down, down I come like glistering Phaëton,
> Wanting the manage of unruly jades.

(3.3.177–178)

With Richard's words – words that are more than a little elaborate (camp even in their unnecessary but exuberant performance of ill-founded and ill-advised grandiosity) – I want to move away from just thinking about the stage. In place of a staged performance, I want to imagine two different readers for these lines and two different circumstances in which the act of reading these words turns them into purposeful interpretations, when it makes something happen beyond the act of reading itself.

One of my imaginary readers is the actor (probably Richard Burbage) who first played Richard II when Shakespeare wrote the play.[8] The other reader is a student, either in high school or taking an undergraduate course; they are reading the play as part of their work in an English or literature class. The first was always the person who Shakespeare imagined as the first reader of his words; the second situation is the one in which his plays have most often been read since Shakespeare first formed a significant part of Anglophone educational curricula. For both readers, the words of the play are a launchpad for subsequent activity: for one, a performance or series of performances and for the other, the outcome is likely to be a number of instructional tasks that are designed to culminate in a written assessment that reflects back on those tasks. The standard form has long been, and still remains, the student essay or exam paper.

The two different sets of goals held by the two seemingly different readers are likely to lead them towards emphasising very different aspects of Richard's short speech. The typically ornate language employed by the

---

[8] Forker, 'Introduction', 122.

defeated king will lead the student, possibly via the notes in their edition or through information provided by a teacher, to the striking simile where Richard compares himself to the son of Apollo: 'like glistering Phaëton'. In what ways, such a reader might ask, is either Shakespeare or Richard thinking about this situation as comparable to the story of Phaëton? Shakespeare's further elaboration of the comparison ('wanting the manage of unruly jades') would draw this reader's attention to the details of the story in which Apollo's foolish son takes out his father's chariot but can't control the horses that help to pull the sun across the sky. He ends up being killed by Zeus, who is trying to make sure the young thief doesn't crash and set fire to the whole world. If Richard is Phaëton, is he foolish to draw our attention to how foolish he is? And are the rebels supposed to be the 'unruly jades'? If so, then 'jades' is an interesting choice in that it can be a word for prostitutes or a pejorative term for older women as well as a dismissive term for useless horses.[9] There is a lot going on with the simile.

And, yet, for all the ambiguities of the allegory that Richard is using to describe his own situation, the exam answers and essays write themselves, don't they? It is all there: narrative direction connects with a key theme (pride and incompetence coming before a fall); imagery (more associations between sovereignty and blinding ('glistering') light); character (Richard's flawed idealism and self-belief); and cultural context (the Renaissance use of classical exemplars). It is a gift of a quotation for any student or essay writer.

To consider that other reader for a moment, however: the 1590s actor reading these lines for the first time, and preparing to speak them on stage.

---

[9] 'Manage' is also an interesting word in this context. Its reference is likely to be to the idea of 'manège', the gentlemanly capacity to control a horse, within the traditional disciplines of horsemanship. Who has been ill-trained here? Richard or the rebels? Shakespeare makes a play on the dual meaning of 'jade' in *Henry V* when the Dauphin and the Constable of France foolishly and boastingly compare horses and mistresses on the night before battle: 'DAUPHIN: Be warned by me then: they that ride so [in the style of an Irish soldier], and ride not warily, fall into foul bogs. I had rather have my horse to my mistress. CONSTABLE: I had as lief have my mistress a jade.' (3.7.45–47)

I want to say that it does not matter at all whether that actor understood the complex networks of references that spin off in multiple directions from Shakespeare's and Richard's simile. I would not want to suggest that the necessary classical learning or political theory was not at the actor's disposal; it almost certainly was. But for him to get what he really needed as a bare minimum from the speech, the network of simile, metaphor, imagery, and intercultural references was not at all important beyond having to learn to repeat the words.

What would have been important, however, would have been the four words that I haven't touched on just yet: 'Down, down I come'. These four words would have provoked the original actor's most important response to the part that he had been given to learn. If the actor read *these* words but somehow failed to make sense of them, or if he did not translate them into action during the performance, then the whole scene would fail or, at least, risk becoming meaningless. In learning them before the performance, he also learns that he is obliged to make a certain movement on stage; he has to descend. This kind of 'clue', built into the dialogue, is sometimes called an 'implied stage direction'.[10] Not just a metaphor, his descent down to Bolingbroke's level must be realised in the performance.

It is with these two lines that I habitually introduce a series of Shakespeare workshops that I have run as part of the University of Sydney's various outreach programmes over the last few years, and that started life in the project described in the Preface. In Section 2, I will provide more descriptive details of those workshops, including the opening spiel around this particular implied stage direction. Here, though, I would just want to say something of the workshops' general purpose which has always been to introduce an alternative mode of reading for various of our

---

[10] For a fascinating account of how these might be used in one form of workshop teaching of Shakespeare, see Caitlin West, 'Implied Stage Directions in Shakespeare: A Workshop Approach', *Metaphor* 2 (2021), 24–28. West's work highlights the ways in which contemporary theatre practitioners might sometimes need to resist what they are being told to do in these implied stage directions. My own approach to their use in workshops is slightly different, as will be seen in subsequent sections.

Shakespeare students, one that mimics the Duke of York a little less and that imitates the actor preparing himself to play the part of Richard a little more. One way that I explain this to myself (and occasionally to students) is that this is a mode of reading that understands the text of the play as less like a crossword clue (where the meaning is always located elsewhere) and more like a list of instructions that contains, within itself, the capacity to generate new meanings.

York, the character, reads the scene in front of him but he seems already to know what it might mean. What he does is explain it for his audience in a way that brooks no disagreement. The explanation that he offers might be at some remove from any direct experience of what is happening, but it draws one part of the evidence of the scene (Richard's eyes) into a powerful and seemingly comprehensive interpretation. Is it even as though he is already writing an essay about the scene, as he confidently relates apparent evidence to assured interpretation?

Sometimes I wonder if I behave a little too much like York as a teacher: 'Here, look at this bit of text; *this* is what it means.' For the most part when I do something like that, I am probably not wrong or, at least, interesting enough to engage students' attention with the text in question and with whatever context I am adducing to make sense of it. York-like, I can bring a mixture of experience, training, and expertise to bear on the act of interpretation and sell this to an audience, defining the experience of reading for them, all without revealing that a sleight of hand is likely to be taking place in which, York-like, I am producing the evidence almost as much as I am providing the interpretation.

This Element, however, is about risking the possibility that I and my students might sometimes be allowed to get things 'wrong' or, rather, be allowed to construct interpretations that are not quite so certain about where they are headed, where a framework for understanding has not yet been put in place. For that to be allowed to happen, I need not to be quite so authoritative as a teacher or so overweening in my interpretative capacities as York.

I choose this speech from *Richard II* as an introductory scene for my workshops mostly for its utility in the demonstrable way that it demands different kinds of reading activity in a short and readily understood piece of dialogue. It provides an obvious example of an implied stage direction alongside some very convoluted figurative language. But I have other reasons for choosing this section of dialogue, reasons that I have never made clear to my colleagues but that extend beyond its practical convenience. These reasons have, though, guided me in my thoughts as I've attempted to think about what it might mean for somebody working in an elite institution like the University of Sydney (the oldest university in Australia, a sandstone cultural icon) to be asked to deliver classes on Shakespeare to school communities that have been habitually and systematically excluded from its cultural privileges along lines of class, culture, and race.

This scene from *Richard II* is a scene of deposition in which the capacity to determine the meaning and purpose of the world is under contention. 'Such is the breath of kings' (1.3.208), Bolingbroke says earlier in the play, commenting on Richard's ability to reduce his sentence of exile with just a single word. But eventually Richard has to give up his crown, albeit *extremely* reluctantly. In disavowing some kinds of authority in the Shakespeare classroom, I am trying to be a little less reluctant in my search for a pedagogy that relinquishes some of its self-authenticating capacities to make sense of the world. I need to disavow my own authority in the Shakespeare classroom in order to make room for students to make sense of their work for themselves. In Section 1, I look at a typical assessment exercise in current Shakespeare teaching, how it might produce a deficit model of teaching and learning, and what further might be learnt from disavowing the kinds of authority that infer something lacking – a deficit – on the part of our students.

1 'Well, sit we down': Disavowing Explanations

Horatio. Well, sit we down,
And let us hear Barnardo speak of this.
Barnardo. Last night of all,
When yond same star that's westward from the Pole
Had made his course t'illume that part of heaven
Where now it burns, Marcellus and myself

The bell then beating one —
Enter Ghost
Marcellus. Peace, break thee off.
(*Hamlet* 1.1.32–38)

These few lines from the opening scene of *Hamlet* are not a passage that high school or undergraduate students would typically spend any time considering when they are 'doing' *Hamlet* as part of their English or Shakespeare classes. The lines do not obviously reference the themes or ideas with which their classes are likely to be concerned. Even though this dialogue contains the exact moment when the ghost of Hamlet's father makes its very first appearance, there does not seem to be anything in the dialogue of the three night-time watchers that is obviously or readily 'quotable' for an essay on the range of questions to which a lot of work on Shakespeare at this level still attends: the depiction of corruption at the Danish court; or the nature of tragedy; or the way that plot relates to character; or how Hamlet's 'delay' might relate to philosophical doubts; or the relationship of the play to film and other adaptations. Neither is it a piece of dialogue that noticeably traces the significant power dynamics that are at work throughout *Hamlet* along lines of gender, race, sexuality, and religion.[11]

---

[11] Scholarship on gender and sexuality in *Hamlet* has a long and various history, perhaps most often associated with psychoanalytic criticism on the play. The opening chapter of Valerie Traub's book *Desire and Anxiety* considers the way in which sexuality genders the female body in *Hamlet* as well as other of Shakespeare plays (Valerie Traub, *Desire and Anxiety: Circulations of Sexuality in Shakespearean Drama* (London: Routledge, 1992)). Work on race in the play is comparatively more recent and has received a boost from the enjoinders of critical race theory to consider whiteness as a category that is far from neutral. As an example of this emerging body of scholarship, see R.M. Christofides, 'Hamlet versus Othello: Or, Why the White Boy Keeps Winning', *Shakespeare* 17.1 (2021), 6–14. On the implications of critical race theory for teaching early modern literature, see David Sterling Brown, '(Early) Modern Literature: Crossing the Color Line', *Radical Teacher* 105 (2016), 69–77. There is a very long history of criticism that puzzles over the difficulties of religious belief in *Hamlet*, a play that seems to veer wildly between expressing Catholic and Protestant

You could stretch the point if you wanted. Perhaps Horatio's companionable interactions with Barnardo and Marcellus represent an ideal and egalitarian male friendship that, in the early modern period, can sometimes instantiate an ideological resistance to centralising forms of sovereignty at the same time as they exclude both women and lower status men from their purportedly more open modes of politics and sociability.[12] From this, we might compare the moment to the other scene that features men at work: the gravediggers. Here, we might notice that they, unlike their noble counterparts, are not able to put their work on hold in quite the same way. But is that a bit too much to read into Horatio's innocuous but welcoming phrase, 'Well, sit we down'? Now I've written it out, I am not entirely sure that it is too much. I have almost persuaded myself that this would be an excellent basis for an essay on *Hamlet*. But isn't that the problem with the plausibility of explanatory frameworks? They are compelling precisely in their capacity to harness evidence to their explicatory juggernaut.

Or maybe with this passage there is also an opportunity to do something slightly more formalist or even metadramatic. Perhaps it is possible to understand this passage as typical of the dilatory progression of the play's narrative. The three watchmen are supposed to be watching out either for Denmark's enemies or for a nightly spectral apparition but what do they do? They take their eyes off whatever might be arriving over the horizon and they sit down, all the better to listen to each other telling stories. As watchful guardians of Denmark's national security, they make great fireside storytellers. Barnardo even adds extraneous details ('When yond star that's westwards from the pole . . . The bell then beating one') in the best tradition

orthodoxies. Michael Neill's book *Issues of Death* is a good way into the implications of this indecision (Michael Neill, *Issues of Death: Mortality and Identity in English Renaissance Tragedy* (Oxford: Oxford University Press, 1997)).

[12] See Laurie Shannon, *Sovereign Amity: Figures of Friendship in Shakespearean Contexts* (Chicago and London: The University of Chicago Press, 2002). For a more general account of friendship in *Hamlet*, see Arthur C Evans, 'Friendship in *Hamlet*', *Comparative Drama* 33.1 (1999), 88–124.

of the tall tale.[13] Just as they do sit down, they are interrupted by the ghost: 'the time', as Hamlet later tells us, 'is out of joint'. The play's haunted and haunting approach to narrative progression is available right from these early sections of dialogue and stage business. But again, if I were a student who had a short essay to write on, for example, action and inaction in the play, I might not select this moment as one of my most pertinent examples of the play's compulsion to go on small detours. There are much bigger and more significant detours ahead.

Thematic or formal concerns are, of course, not the only areas within which study of Shakespeare might currently take place in high school and undergraduate classes, but these kinds of questions do often still dominate exam papers and curricula and also, therefore, classroom discussions and pedagogical approaches. In my home state of New South Wales in Australia, *Hamlet* was examined as part of the 'Advanced English Course' until 2016, part of the 'Critical Study of Texts'.[14] The question in the HSC (High School Certificate) English exam in 2016 was, 'How does Shakespeare use imagery to portray challenging ideas about truth and deceit in *Hamlet*?'[15] This is a fairly typical question of the kind asked by high

[13] Catherine Belsey locates this moment in the play, and the presence of the ghost more generally, in a tradition of 'winter tales': 'On a dark winter night, then, three seated figures are absorbed by a ghost story. Among the terms in circulation in the period for far-fetched narratives and improbable fables, one favourite was "a winter's tale." In the long, cold evenings, when the soil had been tilled to the extent that climatic conditions permitted, the still predominantly agricultural community of early modern England would sit and while away the hours of darkness with fireside pastimes, among them old wives' tales designed to enthral young and old alike'. (Catherine Belsey, 'Shakespeare's Sad Tale for Winter: *Hamlet* and the Tradition of Fireside Ghost Stories' *Shakespeare Quarterly* 61.1 (2010), 4).

[14] Many thanks to my colleague, Jackie Manuel, for helping me navigate the sometimes baroque requirements of the high school curricula. *Hamlet* is still on the syllabus but now only as a text in one elective ('Elective 4: Literary Mindscapes') within the more marginal, Extension 1 Elective, something that is taken by fewer students.

[15] HSC English Advanced Examination (2016), Paper 2, Module B, Question 3.

school exams or undergraduate essays, and not, I think, necessarily or intrinsically unproductive. The journey from reading to interpretation invited by a question like this is complex, appropriately so for the senior level at which it was pitched. Abstract ideas ('truth' 'deceit') are tied to specific, observable aspects of the text ('imagery') and a relationship between the two is understood as eliciting a specific response ('challenging'). Answering this would require a lot of careful and well-informed navigation through the play and is potentially a worthwhile journey for students to embark upon. Detailed answers to this kind of question would have to be the result of hard work (collaboratively on the part of students and teachers) and of rigorous thinking, although by insisting on the play's 'ideas' being self-evidently 'challenging' the question is presupposing some part of the students' work. (What if we wanted to think of Shakespeare as quietist and conservative rather than 'challenging' in his presentation of ideas?) Shakespeare's language ('imagery') is notoriously thick with often polysemic metaphors and other figures of speech. To parse this aspect of the dialogue whilst also thinking about how complex networks of figuration relate to abstract ideas is both the lifeblood of this kind of question and often an extraordinarily rewarding activity. I even think that this kind of question is, to some extent, built into the way that Shakespeare writes; his knotty language regularly imbricates the abstractly metaphysical with the doggedly material within densely and idiosyncratically figurative dialogue. This aspect of his writing is what Simon Palfrey identifies as 'Shakespeare's habit of concentrating possibilities into single moments'[16] Shakespeare writes really strangely; addressing that strangeness and working out where the metaphors might lead is a large part of how rewarding an experience it is to read Shakespeare. (Contrary to popular opinion, is it really the case that Shakespeare's plays come alive on the page much more than they do on the stage?)

How, though, does literary study – set up for students in the way indicated by such exam questions – tend to work? The plays are often situated (by the questions, the syllabi, by the teachers, by model answers

[16] Simon Palfrey, *Shakespeare's Possible Worlds* (Cambridge: Cambridge University Press, 2014), 11.

to essays, and in the minds of students) in contexts (thematic, historical, ideological, and theoretical) that are construed, in various ways, to make sense of the texts. They offer horizons of understanding against which the evidence of the plays is silhouetted by explanation. Although claims could be made that the relevant themes and ideas have themselves been derived from a careful reading of the texts, in practice the explanatory frameworks tend to come in advance of the act of reading, providing guidance within an overall task of taming the plays into more pliable states of being.

These processes of contextualisation do important work; they provide platforms for conversations to take place between students and teachers and out of these conversations, opportunities for students to develop and demonstrate their interpretative skills as they relate appropriate textual evidence to explanatory contexts and frameworks. That is, there is a clear heuristic value to limiting the scope for interpretations within the classroom setting. Aiming towards exam questions like the *Hamlet* question quoted above can be an exemplary and generative way for literary studies to provide a home in the school or university curriculum for speculative thought. It is entirely possible for this activity to provide opportunities for the best of what we would expect in a literature classroom or tutorial, and for the kind of teaching that, for example, Robert Eaglestone celebrates when he identifies the necessarily discursive nature of literary study, offering 'a sense of dialogue' wherein our English lessons 'overflow the more constrained categories of knowledge', connecting individual response to other kinds of knowledge in dialogues that should, in theory, be both endless and inclusive.[17]

Unfortunately, the writing prompted by this kind of essay question does not always (or often?) rise to the challenge of making those connections in substantial ways. The barriers to interesting work that can be built into this kind of approach are readily seen in an exemplary response to the HSC Hamlet question, the response offered as a study aid in the publicly available webpages of TSFX, a tuition provider for senior high school students in Australia. This answer is held up as an ideal form which students might

[17]   Robert Eaglestone, *Literature: Why It Matters* (Cambridge: Polity, 2019), 51.

adapt to other questions on their Shakespeare texts. This model answer to the *Hamlet* question ties itself in knots as it attempts to display as much knowledge as possible whilst also referencing a range of evidence from the text. Doing both of those things is an essential part of garnering good marks. But, as a result of these imperatives, most of the argument in the essay is constructed out of attempts to extrapolate abstract concepts from the material evidence of the play's language, often in a manner that stretches logic. So, for example, we get sentences like this: 'Early on, Hamlet recognises a tension between the burgeoning secular humanism of the Renaissance and the entrenched religious orthodoxy, as his desire to "drink hot blood" is tempered by a "dread of something after death".'[18] In TSFX's account of *Hamlet*, the character of Hamlet becomes a spokesperson for the play's presupposed thematic content and the essay breathlessly moves from observation to conclusion without showing us how or why these connections might work or make sense. In the process, the young prince has become aware of both 'secular humanism' and the 'Renaissance'. It might be quite right for us to situate the play in this kind of cultural history – of course it is – but it is not right to suggest that the play or its characters are, themselves, aware of their place within it. The writing has decided, beforehand, what *Hamlet* is 'about' and has then gone about looking for aspects of the text that fit that assumption. This practice leads to the logical impasses in which the essay finds itself. Perhaps it is the case that somebody like Hamlet would have personally borne witness to interna-tional sociocultural shifts and represented them through means of oblique figurative language. But it seems unlikely. In its rush to turn Shakespeare's language into evidence for a pre-planned essay on historical context, the writer misconstrues the representational strategies of literary texts. Moreover, as a means to paper over these epistemological cracks, the essay finds itself having to deploy outdated explanatory models such as

---

[18] TSFX (The School for Excellence), 'How Does Shakespeare Use Imagery to Portray Challenging Ideas about Truth and Deceit in *Hamlet*?' (www.tsfx.edu .au/resources/how-does-shakespeare-use-imagery-to-portray-challenging-ideas-about-truth-and-deceit-in-hamlet/)

the 'Great Chain of Being', treating such concepts as self-evident back-grounds that make sense of the essay's own leaps of analysis.[19]

Model answers like this essay on *Hamlet* serve a distinct purpose. They provide frameworks for understanding that quieten and control the evidence, preparing concepts to be readily learned, repeated, and re-applied when a slightly different question is asked. In this kind of writing, a platform is laid for the safe and transparent display of second-hand knowledge. The essential message that is transmitted by this work is that all evidence from the text is interchangeable. Literary texts cease to be the idiosyncratic things that they are and start to behave in an orderly fashion, falling in as evidence behind a distinct and applicable argument. However, with such overarching explanations, all words can be made to fit and I would argue that there is little real understanding of the play's 'imagery' or other aspects of its language as these get turned into ciphers for predetermined ideas. The practice of reading is reduced to the forensic process of spotting evidence for a predetermined solution. What can be seen in this essay is not the productive dialogue between response and knowledge that would be the hallmark of the best literary study at these levels, and this is because students are not necessarily afforded the space to test the assumptions that lie behind the knowledge that they are, nevertheless, asked to reproduce. Liam Semler has described some of the pitfalls of Australia's highly systematised approach to education and to literary study in particular. Of Stage 6 Shakespeare study (Years 11 and 12, their final years of high school) Semler writes that '[a]n important reservation ... is that in most cases teachers must teach and students must learn the plays in relation to pre-defined thematic frameworks'.[20] By skewing

---

[19] Popularised by E. M. W. Tillyard in his wartime classic of literary and cultural criticism, *The Elizabethan World Picture* (London: Macmillan 1942), the idea that classical and medieval philosophies of order maintained a compelling and all-encompassing hold not just over Elizabethan and Jacobean understandings of the world but also over everyday means of expression (including drama) has had a much longer life in high school Shakespeare teaching than it has elsewhere in the world of Shakespeare studies.

[20] Liam Semler, *Teaching Shakespeare and Marlowe: Learning versus the System* (London: Bloomsbury, 2013), 28.

assessment tasks towards replicating interpretative frameworks, the skills of careful, independent reading can readily be thrown out alongside more searching and individual engagements with the texts of the plays. Or, rather, the capacity to display certain aspects of contextual knowledge are privileged, in this kind of work, over developing independent skills in reading, analysis, and interpretation.

One of the things that I am considering in this Element is how such approaches unnecessarily privilege the authorising presence of a teacher or the curriculum that has the teacher as its avatar. This figure is seemingly most in control of the way that the text comes to mean something for the student or the class. Of course, some models for the dissemination of specialised knowledge might be a good thing and the knowledge and expertise of the teacher should not be lightly dismissed. It would surely be important, for example, that students are taught that the representations of women in *Hamlet* are informed by sixteenth-century conceptions of gender and, also, that subsequent performance traditions or critical approaches might either replicate or resist such formulations. Across the enormous reach of current Shakespeare scholarship, the most challenging contemporary readings have emerged from queer scholars and scholars of colour, and it should not be possible to introduce students to Shakespearean texts in the absence of these important perspectives and the knowledge that they have generated. Queer readings of Shakespeare and readings that emerge from the work of premodern critical race studies depend upon the development of expertise and knowledge that exceeds the capacities of any one reader. This critical and generative knowledge is not something that can be retrieved from a direct confrontation with the text but rather requires different kinds of explanatory framework, all informed by collective knowledge, research, and expertise. The importance of placing this knowledge within the context of the introductory Shakespeare classroom should not be understated. Patricia Akhimie, for example, writes about some of the possibilities of an antiracist pedagogy, derived from premodern critical race studies, in the Shakespeare classroom, including the development of collaborative research tasks, with the goal being 'to place the student on the same path and in the same woods in which I found myself when I began asking questions about the significance of race in the Renaissance'[21]. Ambereen Dadabhoy's account of confronting questions of race in the Shakespeare classroom also charges us with adopting specific lenses in order to defamiliarize the texts and make visible their position within longer histories of racial violence.[22] For myself, as a gay man, I often want to situate my own experiences in relation to the material that I am teaching, trying to find productive ways into Alan Sinfield's still-exemplary challenge, a challenge that continues to provoke after all these years: 'How to read *The Merchant of Venice* without being heterosexist.'[23]

The observation I am making of teaching and assessment practices is not, therefore, a call to move towards an anachronistic and implausible new critical turn to the text as the sole generator of its own interpretative possibilities. In a book that I have used since its first publication, finding it to be a galvanising force in various aspects of my teaching, Ayanna Thompson and Laura Turchi make a compelling case for placing discussion within specific, identifiable frameworks as a means 'to organize the class's way through the text'.[24] Their approach is particularly guided by the understanding that we should never assume a culturally neutral ownership of these texts, and never behave as if students bring with them uniform kinds of prior knowledge or skills. Not to provide some kind of lens is, for them, something that would generate the false assumption that the situation of teaching and learning Shakespeare is politically neutral. Thompson and Turchi reject the notion of Shakespeare's supposed universality as an overly

[21] Patricia Akhimie, 'Cultivating Expertise: Glossing Shakespeare and Race', *Literature Compass* 18.10 (2020), 2.

[22] Ambereen Dadabhoy, 'Skin in the Game: Teaching Race in Early Modern Literature', *Studies in Medieval and Renaissance Teaching* 27.2 (2020), 97–111.

[23] Alan Sinfield, 'How to Read *The Merchant of Venice* Without Being Heterosexist' in T. Hawkes (Ed.), *Alternative Shakespeares 2* (London: Routledge, 1996), 135–52. For an interesting take on conjoining Shakespeare teaching with work on contemporary adaptations and queer theory, see Catherine Bates, 'Teaching Queer Theory: Judith Butler, Queer Theory, and *She's the Man*' in Alice Ferrebe and Fiona Tolan (Eds.), *Teaching Gender* (London: Palgrave, 2012), 47–62.

[24] Ayanna Thompson and Laura Turchi, *Teaching Shakespeare With Purpose: A Student-Centred Approach* (London: Bloomsbury, 2016), 26.

simplistic way in which we might try to tie his work to classrooms of diverse students that carries its own prejudices and imbalances. They ask the important question, 'Who benefits from a race-free, gender-free, sexuality and ability-free approach?'[25] The answer is, of course, that it is those people who are not affected by any of these identity markers that are most clearly advantaged by pretending that they don't exist.

The approach I take here does not directly apply questions of identity or marginality to the central western traditions to which Shakespeare is assumed to belong. But neither does it preclude that work. What I am seeking is, rather, a limited intervention that might displace authority from the educator to the student in a small but meaningful way, and purposefully to avoid what Thompson and Turchi identify as 'an inadvertently author-itarian instructional design' that 'operates on the principle that Shakespeare needs to be explained'.[26] The approach to literary study exemplified in the kind of essay-writing task described in this section constitutes an obvious attempt to eliminate risk, to delimit the ways in which literature can be written about in an assessment situation so that both teacher and student feel that they have more control over the outcome. It really, really wants to 'explain'. But reading literature should allow us to be a little bit riskier in the classroom: to risk, in particular, the renunciation of authority, and to move away from knowledge as located in the answers – the essays, the contexts, and the themes – towards education as a form of knowledge production. I am using this Element to imagine one very small way in which this might be happening. One intention is to show the ways in which a seemingly innocuous passage like that quoted at the start of this section might provide as much grist to the young student's mill as any amount of the other more frequently quoted soliloquies and set pieces from the play. Or, rather, that it can be in tackling passages like this, and discovering how they work, that students at the start of their Shakespeare studies might gain some indepen-dent purchase on the task at hand. In the process, I also hope to illustrate ways in which the Shakespeare text might operate within a de-centred classroom, that is a classroom in which the students' generation of

[25] Thompson and Turchi, *Teaching Shakespeare*, 13.

[26] Thompson and Turchi, *Teaching Shakespeare*, 46.

knowledge takes precedence over any instruction coming from the central, authorising figure of the teacher.

'Well, sit we down'. Somehow, even now, after doing it many times, it comes as a revelation to me when I teach *Hamlet* that the night watchmen on the ramparts of Elsinore must sit down at some point during the scene. So much of the opening scene is about looking up, about watching out for who is coming, to the extent that even the audience can seem drawn into its definitive opening question: 'Who's there?' The scene does seem to be all about who sees what and when, and the extent to which what we see can be interpreted, or the extent to which it resists interpretation. But briefly – before he is rudely interrupted by the apparition of the ghost – Horatio leads us in another direction, one where we don't just stand and stare, our hair out on its ends, but where we listen to each other and attempt collectively to make sense of all our experiences. It is in that spirit that I want to move on, in Section 2, to introduce the workshops in a little more detail, starting with some of their theoretical underpinning as well as some more practical details of how they work.

2 Shakespeare and the Ignorant Schoolmaster

Beyond the obvious answer that his plays remain a fixture in most English literature school, college, and university curricula, are there other reasons that make Shakespeare useful in these contexts? One answer is the way that the plays themselves already instantiate a particular kind of pedagogy. The plays demand to be learned in a certain way. Moreover, they demand to be learned in the absence of any guiding or overriding instruction. This means that, because of the way that they are written, the texts of the plays can already constitute a form of de-centred pedagogy. In recent discussions of Shakespeare's texts in the work of theatre historians, particularly in accounts of how the plays were written and shared within companies of players, an understanding of their function has been arrived at which is, for me, uncannily reminiscent of the theories of teaching that emerge from Jacques Rancière's revolutionary account of pedagogy in his classic 1987 text *The Ignorant Schoolmaster*.[27] What these two

---

[27] Jacques Rancière, *The Ignorant Schoolmaster: Five Lessons in Intellectual Emancipation*, Tr. K. Ross (Stanford: Stanford University Press, 1991)

disparate approaches to teaching share is an avoidance of external explanatory authority as a means to generate understanding. In the case of Rancière, that avoidance is elevated to a considered resistance. Rancière understands dominant pedagogical traditions as forms of teaching that work primarily as the movement of knowledge from master to student, and it is these traditions that his work rejects. He writes that '[t]here is stultification whenever one intelligence is subordinated to another', construing the act of teaching as something that subordinates one person (a student) to another (a teacher or master).[28] In place of this 'stultification', Rancière dreams up forms of pedagogy that renounce the authority of the master, replacing them with ways to develop understandings that emerge in the process of reading itself. The question he is asking is whether it is possible to teach without 'subordinating' one intelligence to another. The early modern dramatic text is an example of one instance where this does, indeed, seem to be possible. In this section, I provide a theoretical underpinning for the workshops, and I do this by forging a connection between Rancière's approach to teaching learning and some current scholarship on Shakespearean playtexts.

In thinking about how a play makes its way from script to performance, Tiffany Stern begins with a basic premise. 'Shakespeare', she writes, 'was an actor writing for actors'.[29] That is, Shakespeare wrote his plays knowing that the written words were primarily of use to other actors. Stern elaborates by claiming that Shakespeare 'wrote anticipating the way his texts would be disseminated and learned'.[30] An idea of learning – that the lines would be learned – is a structuring principle of the way that the plays are initially written. They are written to be learned as well as read and the kind of learning involved exceeds merely memorising them. It is not just that they would be learned in order to be repeated – what we normally think of as 'learning your lines'. Actors, rather, were expected to understand something about the whole play from 'learning' their lines. Holger Syme imagines the scene in which this initial encounter with the text takes place, as the actor first gets hold of his

---

[28] Rancière, *The Ignorant Schoolmaster*, 13.

[29] Tiffany Stern, *Making Shakespeare: From Stage to Page* (London: Routledge, 2004), 3.

[30] Stern, *Making Shakespeare*, 3.

lines. 'By Shakespeare's time', he writes, 'the solitary actor preparing his role could have predicted how the play would be staged with some certainty'.[31] The lone actor, faced with his lines, is able to imagine, from the act of reading, at least something about the entire production. In a re-examination of the evidence, Leslie Thomson finds that Stern overstates the case for rehearsals being more or less unnecessary for the early modern stage. Some aspects of the performance, Thomson argues, must have required at least a small group rehearsal. Whilst some extratextual actions are provided for in the implied stage directions of the dialogue, more complex performances such as dumb shows or actions that needed complex blocking mean that 'almost no part could have been adequately prepared and realized by a player until he had rehearsed it with at least some other players'.[32] Even with Thomson's qualifications, however, a great deal of information is present in the dialogue itself and it still constitutes a form of pedagogy aimed at bringing individual players into a collective understanding of what has to happen. And it is a pedagogy specifically designed to work in the absence of the author. The way that the dialogue has to be learned means that this learning extends beyond remembering the words also to encapsulate finding out how to perform a given role within the context of a completed performance, perhaps even something about the overall play and its possible impact on an audience.

This expansive conception of what it means to *learn* the text is built into the process of writing because of the way that companies such as those for which Shakespeare wrote went about their business. In a modern theatre company, a very prominent place is given to the director who is usually the ultimate (York-like?) decision-maker for any production, particularly in terms of set design, blocking, and stage business. Actors may have important contributions to make, derived from their knowledge, skill, and experience. But the overarching plan for any production of the play usually rests with the central, authorising figure of the director. No such job as a director existed in the early modern playing companies and, therefore, if

[31] Holger Syme, 'The Theater of Shakespeare's Time' in *The Norton Shakespeare* (3rd edition), Ed. S. Greenblatt (New York: Norton, 2015), 112.

[32] Leslie Thomson, *From Playtext to Performance on the Early Modern Stage: How Did They Do It?* (New York and London: Routledge, 2022), 52.

a play were to work in performance, what actors had to *do* as well as what they had to *say* needed to be built into the scripts or, at least, into the act of reading the scripts. The skill of the early modern actor rests in large part on their capacity to interpret written text and transform it into complex sets of action.[33] Moreover, as Syme indicates with his picture of the solitary actor learning his lines on his own the night before a performance or even in Thomson's picture of the actor reading in advance of a small group rehearsal, the early modern actor has to be a well-attuned reader with an enviable attention to detail, able to parse and interpret the dialogue in ways that immediately bring it to life in his mind before that initial interpretation is brought together with the parallel work of his acting colleagues. As John Astington describes it, the process of making yourself 'perfect' as an early modern actor was an extraordinarily complex business that involved not only learning your lines but also building an understanding of the location and contexts of those lines within several much larger wholes:

> Yet if study was, at one level, to make one word- and line-perfect, it surely involved a good deal more for actors of some ability and experience. The entire development and emotional contour of a role was contained within a written part. Speeches of any length would have been weighed for their

---

[33] Recent work on the considerable skills that early modern actors would have developed over their careers includes the work that I cite below from Evelyn Tribble on 'entrainment', but also the work of Harry McCarthy on the particular forms of skill that would be associated with boy actors, and Clare McManus on the use of acrobatics on the early modern stage, including female tightrope walkers. Evelyn Tribble, *Early Modern Actors and Shakespeare's Theatre: Thinking with the Body* (London: Bloomsbury, 2017); Evelyn Tribble, *Cognition in the Globe: Attention and Memory in Shakespeare's Theatre* (New York: Palgrave, 2011); Harry McCarthy, '"M[aster] Monkesters Schollars: Richard Mulcaster, Physical Education, and the Early Modern Boy Companies', *Early Theatre* 24.2 (2021), 31–54. The work of McManus on acrobatics is one aspect of the research project, *Engendering the Stage*; her work on female performance more broadly can be found in Clare McManus, '"Sing it like poor Barbary": *Othello* and Early Modern Women's Performance', *Shakespeare Bulletin* 33.1 (2015), 99–120.

rhythms and their structures of thought and feeling; experimental patterns of delivery, subject to careful self-criticism, would have been tried out, like a pianist listening to his or her own playing concurrently with working out the intricacies of the written notes in the score. Imagining oneself into a character and a fictional dramatic experience began with and was continued in the process of learning a part; as an actor one studied more than a sequence of words, unreflectingly, parrot-like, but necessarily one absorbed the entire fiction of which they were to be, on stage, the audible determinant.[34]

I am less convinced than Astington that character arc would be the chief determinant of how the play might be conceived in these circumstances; the practical considerations of gesture, movement, and blocking are more likely to determine character than the other way around. But the sense of an intensely detailed self-directed learning experience is surely right. What is being imagined is a process whereby individual actors locate themselves within the complex machinery of a play and its production on stage. They do this in significant part through the instructions available to them in the script that they are obliged to learn. Inferences are made from this partial evidence and, when put together with all the separate parts, this somehow results in a successful whole. It is like putting together a particularly complex piece of Ikea furniture but with only one page of the manual; you have to hope that your colleagues playing the other parts have learned the other pages and that it will all work once you start fitting it together.

---

[34] John Astington, *Actors and Acting in Shakespeare's Time: The Art of Stage Playing* (Cambridge: Cambridge University Press, 2010), 141. My own amateur attempts at playing the piano would agree with Astington's assessment of the complexity of learning a new piece as an analogy. The trick is, somehow, to stand outside of yourself and observe your own playing as if you were somebody else at the same time as completely inhabiting the body that has, nevertheless and almost without conscious thought, to devote itself entirely to the act of playing the music that is either in front of you or located in your memory.

As the work of Evelyn Tribble and others has demonstrated, for all this to work requires not only highly skilled practitioners but also a well-developed professional system in which actors are able to situate themselves very precisely and with confidence. Theatre historians have established the actor's 'part' as the foundational document in the production of early modern theatre.[35] Individual actors would have received a manuscript that contained only their own words, with perhaps some relevant stage directions. Without a collective rehearsal, a successful performance was, therefore, predicated on the actor's solitary study of this 'part'. Tribble describes and celebrates the skill involved in the early modern actor's cognitive capacities, as he produces a performance out of the initial act of reading:

> The primary cognitive artefact of the player was his individual part, which contained only his own lines and his cues. His preparation consisted primarily of private study of this part, during which time he scanned the part for the changing passions on display and uplifts them into his body – moving them from the language of the playwright through his body and by means of the art of gesture out to the audience.[36]

Tribble uses theories of cognition to make sense of these complex practices and, as a consequence, what she describes is not always a conscious act on the part of the performer. Rather, it is a form of what she calls 'entrainment' in which the actor's capacities to read and translate the text into spoken words and action are placed within extended cognitive capacities that encompass the entirety of the early modern stage, including the other actors, the physical make-up of the stage and theatre, the relationship between performers and audience, and the commercial arrangements of the company and the playhouse. What the individual actor learns to do with each script is likely to

[35] Simon Palfrey and Tiffany Stern, *Shakespeare in Parts* (Oxford: Oxford University Press, 2007). Again, Thomson has questioned the absolute nature of the 'part' as capable of generating a whole performance in the absence of some forms of mediation via group rehearsal.

[36] Tribble, *Early Modern Actors*, 30.

happen automatically, without conscious thought, embedded within the various systems and institutions of early modern theatre.

That this complex act of interpretation happens in the absence of a director and without an author looking over the shoulders of the players makes this situation fascinating as a model for teaching. It looks very much like a pedagogy from which authority has been removed or, at least, removed from a person and located, instead, in the shared object of a written text and in communal (if initially dispersed) acts of reading. There can be no doubt that the playscripts are a form of teaching; they contain within themselves the demand to be learned, for that learning to be complex, and for the resulting knowledge to progress on to other forms of meaning-making. In contemporary teaching practice, we might even see this as a well-designed form of progressive, scaffolded teaching and learning.

I want to return to Rancière; I believe that he imagines a situation that can productively be compared to the inbuilt pedagogical strategies of the original Shakespearean script. In the opening chapters of *The Ignorant Schoolmaster*, Rancière describes a set of events that might be the stuff of nightmares for any teacher, ignorant or otherwise. A lecturer in French literature, Joseph Jacotot, is working at the University of Louvain in 1818. In Rancière's account, he finds himself teaching a class of Flemish students who do not speak any French. He, himself, speaks no Flemish. Jacotot's solution to the seemingly unbridgeable gap between himself and his students is to use a bilingual edition of one of the texts that they were studying, François Fénelon's seventeenth-century novel, *Télémaque*. The decision that he takes to use the parallel text provides Jacotot with the basis of an experiment. The students are asked to read and to make sense of the French novel by means of the Flemish translation and, over a period of weeks, they start to repeat what they have learned in class. The results are many times more successful than the lecturer had imagined, with students developing and demonstrating an understanding of the complex language of the literary text that surpasses students who have been taught by more traditional means. Rancière describes this moment as a 'grain of sand' that has 'gotten into the machine' of traditional teaching.[37]

---

[37] Rancière, *The Ignorant Schoolmaster*, 3.

From this initial experiment, both Jacotot and (after him) Rancière develop a practice and theory of teaching that explicitly rejects mastery in the classroom, embracing an approach that does away with teacherly 'explication' as a primary pedagogical mode:

> The revelation that came to Joseph Jacotot amounts to this: the logic of the explicative system had to be overturned. Explication is not necessary to remedy an incapacity to understand. On the contrary, that very incapacity provides the structuring fiction of the explicative conception of the world.[38]

Rancière construes 'explication' as a teaching activity that, far from drawing student and teacher closer together, rather instantiates a sense of distance between teacher and student that produces the idea and experience of mastery in the first place. Traditional teaching only pretends, in this view, that its aim is to ensure that students reach the same level of expertise or mastery as the teacher; the actual function of explication is to produce differentiation itself. The gap in understanding between master and student is the result of viewing teaching as primarily 'explicative' rather than something that is overcome in the explanation. The traditional version of education is, for Rancière, one in which teaching is understood, at least on the face of it, as a means for the teacher to 'transmit his knowledge to his students so as to bring them, by degrees, to his own level of expertise'. Perhaps this seems like common sense, but what gets missed is the student's lot in this system, something that Rancière describes as an experience of loss or even of grief:

> the child who is *explained to* will devote his intelligence to the work of grieving: to understanding, that is to say, to understanding that he doesn't understand unless he is explained to.[39]

---

[38] Rancière, *The Ignorant Schoolmaster*, 6.
[39] Rancière, *The Ignorant Schoolmaster*, 8.

The main message that a student gets from an explanation is not the content of the explanation but an experience of deficit. By explaining something to a student, I might think that what I am doing is empowering them with new knowledge but, all along, I am just as likely to be disempowering them with a powerful sense of their shortcomings. Some understanding might come along with the explanation, but the overriding experience is one that reinforces hierarchy and division. I have always found the opening phrase of the passage quoted above profoundly moving. As someone caught up in the world of education, I am often worried by the constant hum of low-level dissatisfaction and tension that accompanies the scene of teaching and learning. Much of this generalised affect of resentment can be attributed to the way that together teachers and students devote all our intelligences to the 'work of grieving'. Students too often think that they don't belong, or that they know enough to start speaking. Lecturers assume that their approach to a topic is superior to that of others. To recognise the traditional classroom as, potentially, a site of unresolved grief rather than of care is, I would hope, one step towards a happier classroom. The experiment described by Rancière aims to promote understanding without the burden of mastery and servitude that usually accompanies the otherwise regular reminder that it is the intelligence and knowledge of the schoolmaster that is the gauge against which students' own understanding is measured.

How do Rancière's aspirations for an emancipatory form of pedagogy resemble the systems in place in the Shakespearean theatre? And how might either of these two different pedagogical modes be activated in the contemporary Shakespeare classroom? The most apparent (but not the only) point of contact is the lack of 'explication'. Jacotot's students gain understanding from their own (initially solitary) work with the printed parallel texts aiming towards improved facility with the language as the weeks progress; the early modern actor's understanding of the play in which they are due to act is derived not from a director or even directly from the playwright but from the text of the play and their growing capacity to make sense of its multiple requirements. The technology at the heart of both is the book (the actor's 'part' or the translated novel), another point of contact between the two practices that is at least as interesting as the absence of authority. Rancière asks about the teacherly impulse to provide masterly explanations: 'But why should the book need help?'[40] By refusing to step in with an explanation before the student/actor starts reading a text, by withholding an explanation of what the book really 'means', the skills of reading that the text requires are developed in a way that does not seem like it is addressing a deficit and, importantly, does not, as an integral structural feature, reinstate relations of mastery, servitude, authority, and grief. Does this seem unrealistic with Shakespeare's plays in the twenty-first century, accustomed as we are to the multiple glosses, crib notes, and textual criticism with which they are surrounded?

In the context of the outreach programmes that I describe in more detail in the next section, the Shakespearean text does not just provide a point of contact between the two shared curricula of the high school and the university. The texts also offer an opportunity (perhaps only for a brief moment and not always entirely successfully) for an abdication of authority. This is important to me in this context because of the potential that clearly exists for producing circumstances that merely reproduce a sense of deficit on the part of the visiting students. And this was exactly what we wanted to avoid. To invite students to the university campus in order to explain something to them would, for me, have been unconscionable, producing nothing more than a belief on the part of the students that they had no agency in their own learning, that they required being explained to by somebody like me, with all the privilege of the University of Sydney behind me. I would argue, however, that these considerations can have a relevance that extends beyond the circumstances of these outreach workshops. In the workshops that I describe in the next three sections, I started some work that I have also sometimes translated into other teaching circumstances with other cohorts of students. But first, I want to consider what we did in the project. The first workshop that I describe deals with the scene in *King Lear* when Gloucester has his eyes plucked out, and with students solving the problem of how to do this on stage with little more than the text of the scene in front of them.

---

[40] Rancière, *The Ignorant Schoolmaster*, 4.

3 How to Gouge Out Some Eyes: A Workshop Approach

In the first large campus visit of our programme, we set aside a good part of the afternoon to a Shakespeare learning activity. After a brief set-up from me, students worked in groups on a particular challenge and then we came back together to compare notes and, to some extent, do a small 'performance', although it was stressed throughout that nobody was being asked to 'act' in any way that was either convincing or competent. This is certainly not another manifesto for performance-based Shakespeare teaching, especially if such an approach is imagined as dismissing or belittling the act of reading as the core skill and activity of literary studies. The focus (my focus, at least) was on reading and understanding the text rather than performing it. I opened with a few broad stroke parameters for the subsequent activity: that there was no director in Shakespeare's theatre; that actors had to learn what to do as well as say from reading their scripts; and they did not necessarily need to know the rest of the play in order to make sense of the sections in which they were acting. Some sense of the bare boards of the Shakespearean stage was also provided: that there was not much by way of scenery or props, and that it featured a stage that extended into the audience. I used the small piece of dialogue from *Richard II* as my illustration of how text might be read in order to produce action. Whenever I have done this, both in the first version of the workshops and on subsequent occasions, I have drawn attention to how odd it is to say something like, 'Down, down I come'. 'Nobody', I say, 'would say something like, "Across the room I walk"'. My intention is to highlight those aspects of the text that might stand out as particularly interesting in the coming exercise. With my undergraduate classes, we might supplement this first introduction with Tribble's reading of Thomas Heywood's 1612 *Apology for Actors* that, 'In Heywood's account, the actor's part of speech is the verb – he walks, speaks, acts, tramples, rides, conquers, hews, hunts, fights, murders, kills and, finally, inscribes the pyramids themselves.'[41] In the large-scale school workshops,

---

[41] Tribble, *Early Modern Actors and Shakespeare's Theatre*, 29. The, perhaps unexpected, reference to the 'pyramids' is because Heywood uses an actor performing the part of Hercules as his example, an imagined performance that concludes with Hercules scaling the pyramids and writing, 'Nil ultra' (No more).

however, it is enough to underline the particular relevance of verbs to actors learning their parts.

Following the introduction, I set up the exercise itself as an experiment whereby the students are tasked with finding the solution to a difficult problem in the world of Shakespeare: how to stage the eye-gouging scene in *King Lear*. As with all good experiments, it was important to emphasize that there are no predetermined results, that I have no 'answer book' and that the process is more important than anything. Written instructions, including the text itself, were handed out in small groups and, with some very light-touch supervision from colleagues in each of the groups, the students set about the task.

It is true, I suppose, that this is not quite the 'ignorant schoolmaster' approach in the purist sense that might be imagined. There is too much work on framing for that to be the case. However, the motivation behind the introductory information and instructions is the provision of a level-playing field from which to move forwards, rather than any sense that students are there to learn directly from me or from the other teachers when it comes to the substantive part of the task. One important starting point for the reading activity, then, was that we should all try to approach the script as something more like a list of instructions than a crossword clue. In the latter, meanings are always located elsewhere and our capacity to locate them is dependent on our overarching control of the language and knowledge systems in which they are located. In the former, meaning is generated by how we read what is in front of us and what we might do as a result of that reading. Rather than continue to describe the activity here, I have transcribed the workshop materials in the following order:

 i. Some preliminary notes (mostly for guiding the activity supervisors);
 ii. The scene with some additional notes;
iii. Some questions to guide the groups' responses. These contain three 'decision points', again in support of a sense of agency rather than to test knowledge; these were decisions that the students were to make on the basis of their reading.

The following is a slightly amended transcription of the workshop materials:

Some preliminary notes

The *King Lear* Experiment
Or, 'How to Gouge Out an Eye and Live to Tell the Tale'

In this exercise, what we are trying to do is to work out the relationship between the words that Shakespeare wrote for his characters to speak, and the various actions, gestures, and props that might have brought them to life on the stage of the time. We can do this by experimenting with the words and the space of the stage.

There are no 'right' or 'wrong' answers here. Well, not at the start. What we are trying to do – collectively – is discover what might have been possible. This helps us get to the heart of how the scene might have worked and, if we were studying this scene or play any further, give us a good starting point for further analysis.

On the next pages, you'll find the scene we are looking at. It's a famous scene from Shakespeare's *King Lear*, in which one character, Gloucester, has his eyes plucked out. It is famous partly because it is so difficult to imagine it being staged.

i. The scene with some additional notes

The Scene
Act 3, Scene 7, Lines 29–108

In this scene of the play (Act 3, Scene 7), Gloucester, the faithful friend of the old king, King Lear, has been arrested for giving him assistance. Regan, the old king's daughter, is now in power with her sister, Goneril. They have thrown their father out into a wild storm. Now, with her husband, Cornwall, she is about to interrogate Gloucester about his association with the old King. In the process, they blind Gloucester by gouging out both his eyes.

This is a famous scene from the play, not only because it is particularly gory (and it *is* one of the goriest scenes in a Shakespeare play) but also because it is notoriously difficult to stage: how do you gouge an eye out on stage? How do you do it twice?

By reading the dialogue alongside the picture of the Globe theatre, at the same time as thinking about what kinds of action and gesture would accompany the dialogue, we can experiment with how the play might have come to life and what the effects of this might have been. There are no right and wrong answers here – at least not initially. We are just trying collectively to run an experiment to see how this bit of the play works. The questions below the dialogue are designed to help you make two or three key decisions. There is also a short glossary, after the scene, to help with any tricky words.

People in the Scene

Already on Stage

Regan. Daughter to the old King Lear. Together with her sister Goneril, she has taken control of King Lear's household, throwing him out onto the moor.

Cornwall. This is the Duke of Cornwall, Regan's equally ambitious husband

Other People Who Come into the Scene

Gloucester. This is the Earl of Gloucester. He is a faithful friend to the old King Lear and he has been helping him. He has, though, been betrayed by one his sons to Regan and Cornwall who now want to question him.

Servants. They bring Gloucester onto the stage but, later in the scene, play quite an important role.

King Lear
Act 3, Scene 7, Lines 29–109

TIP

Don't read through the scene from start to finish without stopping.
Have a go at answering the questions, interrupting yourselves as you go along.
The exercise will work better that way.

Enter Gloucester and Servants

CORNWALL Who's there? The traitor?
REGAN Ingrateful fox! 'Tis he.
CORNWALL Bind fast his corky arms.   30
GLOUCESTER What means your graces?
  Good my friends, consider you are my guests:
  Do me no foul play, friends.
CORNWALL Bind him, I say.
REGAN Hard, hard. O, filthy traitor!   35
GLOUCESTER Unmerciful lady as you are, I'm none.
CORNWALL To this chair bind him. – Villain, thou shalt find –
GLOUCESTER By the kind gods, 'tis most ignobly done
  To pluck me by the beard.
REGAN So white, and such a traitor?   40
GLOUCESTER Naughty lady,
  These hairs which thou dost ravish from my chin
  Will quicken and accuse thee.

[I've edited out some of the longish interrogation here; we are interested in turning the words of the scene into movements and gestures.]

                  I shall see   72
  The wingèd vengeance overtake such children.
CORNWALL See't shalt thou never. Fellows, hold the chair. –
  Upon those eyes of thine I'll set my foot.   75
GLOUCESTER He that will think to live till he be old,
  Give me some help! O cruel! O you gods!
REGAN One side will mock another: th'other too.
CORNWALL If you see vengeance –
SERVANT Hold your hand, my lord: 80
  I have served you ever since I was a child.
  But better service have I never done you
  Than now to bid you hold.
REGAN How now, you dog?

SERVANT If you did wear a beard upon your chin,   85
   I'd shake it on this quarrel. – What do you mean?
CORNWALL My villain?
SERVANT Nay then, come on, and take the chance of anger.
REGAN Give me thy sword. A peasant stand up thus?
   Kills him
SERVANT O, I am slain! My lord, you have one eye left   90
   To see some mischief on him. O!
CORNWALL Lest it see more, prevent it. Out, vile jelly!
   Where is thy lustre now?
GLOUCESTER All dark and comfortless.

[Some dialogue edited out here]

REGAN Go thrust him out at gates, and let him smell   103
   His way to Dover. *Exit a Servant, with Gloucester*
   How is't, my lord? How look you?   105
CORNWALL I have received a hurt: follow me, lady, –
   Turn out that eyeless villain: throw this slave
   Upon the dunghill. – Regan, I bleed apace:
   Untimely comes this hurt. Give me your arm. *Exeunt.*

Short Glossary

Ingrateful. Ungrateful.

Corky. Dry, withered up. (Why does Cornwall describe Gloucester's arms like this?)

Naughty. This had a stronger meaning when Shakespeare was writing. It means something more like 'wicked.'

Quicken. Grow. Gloucester means that the cut-off hairs of his beard will come to life!

Wingèd vengeance. Punishment from the gods.

Vile jelly. He means Gloucester's eye.

Lustre. Shine.

Dover. A town on the south coast of England.

Untimely. At the wrong time.

ii. Some questions to guide the groups' responses:

Group Questions

Here are the questions you should think about in your groups. Pay particular attention to one or two of the 'decision points'. That is what we will focus on most when all the groups come together.

1. When Cornwall says, 'Bind fast his corky arms' (31), who is he speaking *to*, and who is he speaking *about*? What do you think *has* to happen on stage as a result of this command, especially as he repeats it: 'Bind him, I say.'

2. Can you work out, from the dialogue, *where* Gloucester is bound?

3. DECISION POINT 1: Where, on stage, would you place Gloucester and his torturers? Why?

4. When Gloucester says, ''tis most ignobly done / To pluck me by the beard.' (39–40), what has happened and who has done it?

5. After a period of interrogation, Cornwall loses patience with Gloucester's continued loyalty to Lear. He addresses his servants again, asking them to 'hold the chair'. What happens next? How does Cornwall gouge out Gloucester's eyes? Can you work it out from the dialogue?

6. DECISION POINT 2: How would you do this on stage?

Only attempt the next two questions if you have time:

7. Looking at the rest of the scene, can you work out the order in which people fight, die, and have their eyes gouged out? Who does what to whom in the rest of the scene?

8. DECISION POINT 3: How might you stage Cornwall's dying instruction to his wife: 'throw this slave / Upon the dunghill' (107–08)

To Consider

- What do you think you have learned about the scene from trying to make these decisions?

The exercise was necessarily put together in the form of group work because of the time constraints within which we were working and also, of course, to foster a collective agency on the part of the visiting students. We also insisted that our visitors should feel free to reconfigure the rooms and spaces within which they were working and to do this exactly as they wished, re-enforcing the message that the spaces of the university were something that they could, if they liked, call their own. The workshops could equally be based on individual reading of the texts and responses to the questions; it is to that goal of greater independence that subsequent, more extended teaching activities have also worked.

The aim was not to 'teach *King Lear*' or to help with 'doing Shakespeare'. The students were not necessarily studying this particular play at school but were, rather, all studying a diverse array of Shakespeare plays in their different English classes. The typical model for high school students attending a workshop at a university is to offer assistance with revising towards exams, offering a supplement to the work that they do in school. However, we were trying to avoid this sense of filling a perceived 'deficit' in the experience and teaching of the students.

Perhaps the best way of indicating the successful implementation of these strategies would be to provide a counterexample and describe one instance where it did not quite go to plan. I was nervous on the day and did not lead any of the break-out groups myself, choosing instead to hover amongst the groups to see how they were going and whether it was all working. Most were lively affairs. They were perhaps a little halting at first but, once started, the groups seemed to switch with little effort between individual reading, collective reading, and attempts at working out the actions of the scene as they went through the questions. One group, however, was quite different. Popping my head around the door, I saw one of my colleagues wielding a whiteboard marker. An accomplished and compelling lecturer, he had clearly ascertained that the students in his group had no experience of *King Lear* and determined that he needed to supply that information in order for the exercise to work. And, so, he had sketched out a summary of the plot and provided an outline of the familial relationships and conflicts underpinning that plot. I had provided what I thought was *just* enough background for the exercise to make sense but my colleague obviously considered that more was needed for his particular group.

In doing this, he misunderstood (and I hasten to add that this was undoubtedly the result of my failure to provide enough support) the exercise, its impetus, and its imagined outcomes. As a result, the teacher was re-inserted as the primary meaning-maker in relation to the material; what Rancière would call the explicatory function of the teaching situation was re-established, and the relations of master and student reinstated. My heart sank a little as I saw this group. They did seem a little quieter and more quiescent than the other groups, sitting down and dutifully listening to the teacher. The activity was evidently more focused on the work of the university-based instructor than it was on the decision-making processes of the visiting students. But I have to confess that I also cheered a little, seeing this as an interesting test. This outlier group seemed to be a classic example of Rancière's grief-inducing conception of the teacher as one who 'transmit[s] his knowledge to his students so as to bring them, by degrees, to his own level of expertise'.[42] In subsequent years and on subsequent occasions, I have tended to be a little more open with my teaching colleagues about my intentions for the workshops.

Of course, the particular contexts of our outreach programme placed the dynamic of mastery and discipleship into stark relief. The form rather than the content of the teaching was what mattered most in what was conceived of as a barrier-breaking event. That, at the end of the activity, students from all the groups were able to share their understandings with each other was some indication that the technique had worked, especially as this was informed by a careful working through of the dialogue. Most groups put this into practice by staging little bits of the scene. They did not necessarily seek to 'perform' the scene in its entirety but, rather, illustrated how the text might work through reference to short bursts of action. So, for example, a particular, unprompted focus whenever I have done this workshop always ends up being the precise location of the chair on stage (central? back or side to the audience? How does it move when the foot is applied to the eye?). The pedagogical strategies built into the way that Shakespeare writes his plays, in the knowledge that they have to be learned in a certain way, had the capacity to generate understandings that emerged from reading rather than from being 'explained to'. In the next section, I look at two further examples of this kind

---

[42] Rancière, *The Ignorant Schoolmaster*, 8.

of workshop. With both of these cases, I had more time with the students; more emphasis was placed, therefore, on the means by which the students conveyed their understanding of the scenes in question. In both activities (one from *A Midsummer Night's Dream* and another from *Lear*), de-centered collective readings of the texts resulted in short silent 'performances' of the scenes in question. From this, students were able to extract the bare bones of the scene, establishing an understanding of some of the play's tone, its plot and power dynamics in a way that emerged from their own work rather than from any explanatory model. The work of dramatic irony as a key feature of Shakespeare's dramatic writing and strategies also came to the fore in these activities, and I will consider how this might further develop a disavowal of centralising authority in 'learning' Shakespeare.

One last word on the eye gouging. At the conclusion of the exercise, students were asked what they had learned about the play from doing the activity. For most of the students, in the absence of any prior knowledge of the play's plot, its characters, or even its genre, some interesting insights emerged. What this short exercise had established for them (again, from their own work rather than via an overarching explanatory blurb from a teacher) was that the play was about political violence, intergenerational conflict, and the relationships between masters and servants; they also noted the that the role of women in relation to power was likely to be of interest in the play. In an exercise that took just ninety minutes in total, they had learned all this for themselves rather than being provided with an abstracted or explanatory framework. What I had learned was that, sometimes at least, it is best to provide students with tools to read the plays for themselves than it is to provide them with prefabricated frameworks for understanding. I don't know if Rancière or Jacotot would approve but, for me, it marked an important step in what I see as an ongoing disavowal of my authority over student's reading in the Shakespeare classroom.

4 Into the Athenian Forest of Dramatic Irony

Another short scene from *King Lear*, this time from a little earlier in the play: Edmund is discovered by his father in the act of reading a letter. Edmund has already mentioned the letter to us without disclosing its contents ('if this letter speed / And my invention thrive, Edmund the base / Shall to th'legitimate. I grow, I prosper' (1.2.19–21)). Shakespeare's actors would have known to have a 'letter' to hand because of the words 'this *letter*' and the use of the emphatically deictic article ('*this* letter') would indicate a need to make sure that the audience sees it. When Gloucester arrives, he asks his son about the letter. Edmund initially claims that it doesn't exist: 'What paper were you reading?', 'Nothing my lord' (30–31). But Gloucester persists and Edmund eventually hands it over for him to read. Gloucester reads it out loud and discovers apparent evidence that his other son, Edgar, has been writing to Edmund to test his willingness to conspire against their father on the grounds that age should give way to youth, allowing the young to enjoy the benefits of their inheritance before they, themselves, are too old to make use of them properly. The letter is self-evidently fraudulent, composed by Edmund to implicate his brother.

This short and apparently simple piece of action, together with the supporting dialogue, constitutes a multi-layered and complex web of knowledge production. The relationships that are constructed between the dialogue and the action during this scene are probably best characterised as dramatic irony. The full significance of what is happening is not available to at least one of the two characters (Gloucester). And the other character, seemingly in charge of the scene (Edmund), is still rendered profoundly vulnerable to the audience's appraisal of his behaviour. The audience, on the other hand, is kept in the dark first about the contents of the letter and, of course, about the unresolved conflict that arises from its discovery. Compressed within about fifteen lines of dialogue is a concentrated example of how drama often works. More than being a representative dramatic moment, however, the scene also allows us to witness competing attempts to make sense of the spectacle. And, especially in the performance of Edmund, we see somebody who produces meaning by withholding – or feigning to withhold, or showing us that he is feigning to withhold – vital elements of the spectacle. The actor playing Edmund must show the audience that he is reading the letter in a way that Gloucester will see but, also, in a way that at least makes a show of him trying to hide the letter from his father whilst also showing the audience that really he means for him to see it. The perennial theatrical game of 'who knows what?' is being played to maximum, almost farcical, effect. And there's more. It appears – to Gloucester at least – that the secret truth behind all of this action is contained in a piece of paper upon which is written – as far as *we* are concerned – an evident piece of fiction.

Within the narrative development of *King Lear*, this scene is clearly all about Edmund's treachery, as it prepares the way for his later involvement with the rebellion of Goneril and Regan, and the ultimate downfall of Gloucester. But it is also a scene about the location of knowledge and the undecidability of that location (in a dramatic text) somewhere between written text and performed gesture. An awareness of this distribution of knowledge and ignorance is built into the implied instructions that the script leaves for the studious and skilful actor, and, I would argue, for the student attuned to the text in some of the ways that I have been describing so far: scripts as instructions rather than clues, and as having the potential to *produce* meaning rather than as *containing* predetermined meanings.

I used this scene as the basis for a short workshop, another part of our outreach programme, this time a smaller and more focused activity at Bankstown Girls High School in Sydney. Having started with the usual preamble that introduces the idea of implied stage directions, I placed the class in groups of three and asked them to work on this small dialogue. They were not asked to produce anything like a facsimile of the kind of performance that the dialogue demands. Rather, I asked them if they could find a way to mime what happens, rendering the short scene in the briefest of gestures, with the third person explaining to the rest of the class why the two 'mime artists' were making the specific decisions that they had made. Initially this had been, for me, a solution to a concern that I had about asking high school students to speak the words of the play out loud, especially in smaller, potentially more intense groups. Too frequently, this proves an anxious stumbling block in Shakespeare classes, even when most assessments are based on reading and writing rather than on speaking and listening. I can imagine other kinds of workshop that would work towards speaking the lines with various degrees of competence and confidence, but these would be performance-oriented activities rather than the work on literary analysis – on *reading* the texts – that I still wanted to pursue. However, this solution of miming, something that I thought a bit too irritatingly obvious at first, threw up further ideas that have proven helpful in other, subsequent workshops and in other contexts. In particular, the interactions between dialogue, gesture, and audience that lie at the heart of this short scene pointed towards the use of mime as an excellent means to strip scenes back to their bare bones whilst exposing the complex systems of knowledge production upon which they are based. Ironically, miming the scene highlights reading and interpretation in ways that speaking does not always manage. In particular, it ensures that reading is not only done for the kinds of 'crossword clue' reading that I discussed earlier; reading has to be focused and directed. Miming did not prove to be a move away from reading but just the opposite, as students had to find ways to read the text, first, for instructions and then for evidence in support of the choices that they were making. At the start of their work on the play, the exercise would provide an intimate encounter with some of its key elements.

On this occasion, the high school students quickly 'got' the exercise and, with very few prompt questions from me, they produced versions of the scene, together with explanations that drew out the implications of the action. As with the other, larger *Lear* exercise, the point was also to provide students with the means to produce, for themselves, meaningful and exploratory understandings of the scene without too much intervention from me or their teachers. From this activity – regardless of what was some limited prior knowledge or understanding of *King Lear* – they came away with a sense of who Edmund is, derived from their own work on the scene itself. The dialogue was teaching them, rather than me.

This exercise on the short *Lear* scene led to two things: some similar exercises in other contexts and with other plays; and some consideration of the potential for the concept of dramatic irony, an important structuring feature of much of Shakespeare's dramatic work, to intersect with a pedagogy that seeks to disavow centralised authority. Does letting go of a sense of single authoritative perspective on events coincide with a capacity to do away with the teacherly mode that pre-packages meaning for students?

I'll describe one of the similar exercises first. This was not designed for the outreach work that we do, but for tutorial groups in my undergraduate 'Shakespeare' class, at that time listed as 'ENGL 2640: Shakespeare' in the

University of Sydney's catalogue of courses.[43] The students in these groups were, for the most part, second-year undergraduates taking a Shakespeare class either as part of their English major in a general Arts degree or as part of a combined degree in Arts and Education. One of the texts that they study is *A Midsummer Night's Dream*. I incorporated a mime activity into some of our work on this play, focussing on the lengthy scene (usually listed as Act 3 scene 2) in which the four young lovers find themselves lost and confused in the woods outside Athens as they chase each other and both Oberon and Robin Goodfellow apply 'love in idleness' to their eyes. Most weeks in this unit the tutorials are run in what is a standard, conventional way. Readings are set from the plays and also from the critical literature, with the expectation that this will promote a series of ongoing conversations.[44] This traditional approach is intended to build a student's competence in contributing to contemporary Shakespeare studies at an appropriate level, including a facility with debates in contemporary literary criticism. This week we stepped out of this tested and familiar mould. Rather than provide students with a series of readings in preparation for the week's class, they were simply asked to re-read Act 3, Scene 2 of *A Midsummer Night's Dream* (or Scene 5 in the *New Oxford Shakespeare* that we were using). For the purposes of this exercise alone, I forewent the usual annotated text and provided them with a version that contained only the original dialogue and non-editorial stage directions. They were forewarned that this reading would provide the basis of an exercise during the following week's tutorial but also that it would not involve any mind-altering drugs or, indeed, any 'acting'.

The work that we did in class involved finding ways, in groups of about six, very roughly to mime large parts of the scene, translating the instructions of the text into actions. The 'roughness' of these exercises is, for me,

---

[43] This 'unit of study' has, since, been moved to our 3,000-level courses (roughly considered appropriate for third-year undergraduates). The basic information can be found here: www.sydney.edu.au/units/ENGL3713.

[44] Current broad areas include Shakespeare and the figurative; Shakespeare, scepticism and belief; and Shakespeare and the environment. Across all areas, we also look at questions of race, gender, and performance.

part of the point. It is within the difficulty of imagining a classroom to be a theatre, the awkwardness involved in the translation (whiteboards for stage backs; desks for audiences) that thinking might take place. As Ralph Cohen describes it: 'Making the classroom into a rough miniature of an Elizabethan theatre provides teachers and their students with a laboratory in which to run experiments with the text.'[45] The 'roughness' that Cohen describes is important to me, implying, as it does, the joint work that is required – shared by students and teachers – as we collectively re-imagine and repurpose a room for our own needs. As with the shorter *Lear* exercise described in Section 3, this mime was accompanied by rationales that linked the decisions being made to clues from the text: when, for example, a character had to lie down; when another character had to step over a fellow actor seemingly without seeing them; when bodies entered and exited the stage; and even where those exits were likely to be located in relation to the action on stage. As with the *Lear* extract, this scene from *A Midsummer Night's Dream* is a rich example upon which to base this kind of work because of the way that it makes use of complex patterns of knowledge and ignorance. Not even Robin Goodfellow fully understands what is happening throughout the scene.

It is also very funny. Mapping out the key events and the most obvious movements of the first 400 lines of this scene results in the following list:

   i. Robin Goodfellow arrives to confer with Oberon;
  ii. Demetrius and Helena arrive while, looking on, Robin and Oberon see that the two young Athenians are arguing;
 iii. Helena leaves, and then Demetrius falls asleep;
  iv. Oberon sends Robin on another errand and applies love potion to Demetrius' eyes;
   v. Robin comes back;
  vi. Lysander arrives in pursuit of Helena;
 vii. Demetrius wakes up and evidently falls in love with Helena;

---

[45] Ralph Cohen, 'Original Staging and the Shakespeare Classroom' in Millia Riggio (Ed.) *Teaching Shakespeare Through Performance* (Modern Language Society of America: New York, 1999), 81.

viii. The three lovers on stage argue until Hermia arrives;
  ix. They all argue, with Hermia trying physically to hang on to Lysander;
   x. The two men exit together, leaving Hermia and Helena to exchange words;
  xi. Helena leaves on her own;
 xii. Hermia leaves on her own;
xiii. Oberon and Robin are left on stage, confused.

The rest of the scene prolongs this frenetic movement across the stage. The young lovers return and continue their argument without ever really understanding why they are at cross purposes, and the two supernatural characters continue to try to control a scene that they also do not fully understand.

Decision points in the scene – moments that determined how students would realise the scene in mime form – include some very obvious stage directions (e.g. when Demetrius lies down to sleep), implied stage directions (e.g. when Oberon says, 'Flower of this purple dye . . . Sink in apple of his eye' (102–04)), and other more subtle cues for gesture (e.g. deictics such as Demetrius telling Lysander that Hermia is approaching 'yonder'). In the mimes and accompanying explanations at which the groups arrived in class, the near-farcical nature of the movement across stage was brought to the fore, particularly emphasising the comic misunderstandings and misplaced responses that underlie the action of *A Midsummer Night's Dream* at this point. Even though students had not, just a few weeks into the semester, paid a lot of attention to the original staging of Shakespeare's plays, the mimes tended independently to recognise the imperative that the scene has for two doors to be used on stage and, for the most part, for characters to enter through one door and leave through the other, producing a kind of whirling, circular movement that drew in the offstage as a part of the labyrinthine forest of which the onstage action was just one part. The exercise, then, was useful for allowing students to come to an understanding of the physical exigencies of the early modern stage and to do so in a way that was more immediate to their ongoing task of reading the plays than merely, for example, showing them pictures or models of the Globe.

Something more was in evidence, however, than the way that the early modern stage can provide excellent opportunities for confusion and comedy. The nature of the scene, for all of its vibrant humour, offers a view of the Shakespearean and/or dramatic text as a place where it is difficult, if not impossible, to pin down a unitary perspective on events and meanings. The Duke of Kent would, with this scene in front of him, be hard pushed to interpret it for the audience in the strong way that he does for his scene in *Richard II*. The polyvocality of drama is realised in a way that also disrupts any certain hold on what is, or even can be, known by any one character, actor, or audience member.

There is no authoritative version of a scene like this, structured as it is through a profound engagement with dramatic irony. G. G. Sedgewick's classic account of dramatic irony still captures best the peculiar effects of this situation:

> The spectator knows the facts, the people in the play do not. A character's actual situation is one thing, his idea or inter-pretation of it is another; the promise things have for him is at variance with their outcome – they are not what they seem.[46]

This situation is recognisable as constituting the most fundamental experi-ence of watching mimetic drama. Even if it comes to the fore in scenes like these from *Lear* and *Midsummer*, this arrangement underpins all drama that claims to present mimetic action. When watching, the point is that we assume that no one character in a play can know everything. A rush to explain the Shakespearean text within given frameworks can remove some of the energy of this dependence on dramatic irony; it might turn out to be much too Kent-like in its arrogant presumption.

These scenes foreground what is present in almost every aspect of Shakespeare's work for the stage: a dramatic irony that depends on an uneven distribution of knowledge. However, Sedgewick's classic statement falls

[46] G. G. Sedgewick, *Of Irony, Especially in Drama* (Toronto: University of Toronto Press, 1948), 25.

a little short of describing the full effect of scenes like this and of dramatic irony in Shakespeare more generally, where it is often a lot less certain that the audience is fully informed. This is a kind of irony that is not quite like the 'stable irony' described in Wayne Booth's classic account of irony in fictional narratives. Booth describes an ironic aspect to fiction in which readers or audiences have access to more knowledge than anybody else and in which we assume we share that knowledge both with the author and with other readers. Booth's 'stable irony', a feature particularly of prose fiction from the eighteenth century onwards, stabilises interpretation through the revelation of a fixed perspective on events 'in the sense', as he writes, 'that once a reconstruction of meaning has been made, the reader is not then invited to undermine it with further demolitions and reconstructions'.[47] While this does work towards what we all experience as a shared understanding of how specific ironies might work, there is a sense in which drama can never work quite like this, in that knowledge is almost always contingent, withheld to some extent. Characters come on to the stage, but we do not learn their names until somebody else addresses them. If they are addressed by what turns out to be the wrong name (as, for example, in the opening scene of Oscar Wilde's *The Importance of Being Earnest*), we don't even have the security of tying actor to character to name in ways that produce a secure perspective. *Hamlet*'s opening question '[w]ho's there?' is never far away from any theatrical representation of character or event, mostly because it is never fully answered to any complete satisfaction. The dramatic irony which subtends dramatic representation is always a little closer to Booth's 'unstable' ironies to the extent that shared knowledge can never be fully assumed. Booth argues that, in *Twelfth Night*, nobody would ever mistake what is intended by Viola's address to Duke Orsino, when she uses the conditional 'were I a woman'. We know (that she knows that Shakespeare knows) that Viola means to remind us that she *is* a woman and, indeed, that she is in love with Orsino. Such a stable interpretation is dependent, as Booth claims, on 'an absolute sharing of certain knowledge'.[48] And, of course, this is largely right. The play would

---

[47] Wayne C. Booth, *A Rhetoric of Irony* (Chicago: The University of Chicago Press, 1974), 6.

[48] Booth, *A Rhetoric of Irony*, 256.

completely lose meaning if we didn't all collectively remember that Viola was in disguise. However, that is not the same as believing knowledge always to be shared equally, of course across characters but also between the action, the playwright, the characters, and the reader or audience.[49] There is always a little room for ignorance in dramatic texts. And, in teaching, we would be remiss to assume that any knowledge was shared 'absolutely'. Another example of a workshop where mime has colluded well with uses of dramatic irony is one on the banquet scene of *Macbeth*. As students begin to work on piecing this scene together with only the script in front of them, it slowly dawns on all of us that nobody (not any one character, not the audience, not even (perhaps) the author) knows exactly either whether there is a ghost 'really there' or, indeed, who in the scene and audience knows what and when. It is a perfect scene to work on in the disavowal of teacherly authority and of any authoritative perspective on the events and meanings of the play. Knowledge is always uneven and partial, both in the playhouse and in the classroom.

Section 5 looks at an exercise that was based on a scene from *The Winter's Tale*, in which we have a character – Paulina – who tries really, really hard to impose a specific meaning on the visual spectacle in front of us. This exercise was developed within a special project targeting future English teachers who were also English majors taking my undergraduate course. We set up a separate series of workshops, part funded by a grant from the faculty's teaching innovation scheme, that paralleled our work on the plays with a consideration of Shakespeare pedagogy. This series of workshops encountered, perhaps, the limit point of some of the methodologies described so far. These trainee teachers were, despite a willingness to participate and consider the issues, on the whole resistant to the idea of giving up some of their authority as the teacher in the classroom. For me, the closing scene of *The Winter's Tale* and the exercise that we developed around that scene provided an interesting means to reconsider both the role of the 'ignorant schoolmaster' in the Shakespeare classroom and the

---

[49] Even Booth's point misses at least one of the points, which is surely that the actor playing Viola would likely not have thought of himself as female at all.

ongoing possibilities for dramatic irony as a structuring principle for a less authoritarian pedagogy.

5 'It is required': Rubrics, Teacherly Authority, and the Problem with Paulina

The 'statue scene' at the end of *The Winter's Tale* is tightly choreographed. Within the scene, the direction appears to come from Paulina but, for an overall performance of the scene, the detailed instructions are a product of Shakespeare's more than usually emphatic implied stage directions. From Leontes' opening address to Paulina ('O grave and good Paulina!') through to the very last line (also Leontes: 'Hastily lead away'), the dialogue assumes distinct gestures and movements on the part of the actors. In an exercise that formed part of a series of seminars targeted at Bachelor of Education students who were also taking the main 'Shakespeare' unit within the University of Sydney's English curriculum, we worked on this scene in a way that was designed to respond to the numerous cues that are contained in the dialogue. Coming towards the end of the seminar series, students were already familiar with the basics of the stage and with the effects of implied stage directions. The task offered to the students by the text was, therefore, how to make sense of this scene within those already-learned parameters.

The dialogue in that final scene is liberally punctuated by cues for action and clues as to what must happen on stage. It seems that Shakespeare was intent on ensuring that it worked in quite specific ways, writing the basis for all of the scene's gestures and actions into the characters' speeches. One thing that occurs from Paulina's introduction of the statue onwards ('But here it is' (5.3.18)) is that, as a sequence of gestures brings the statue into view, how close to the statue any particular character might be situated is also tightly regulated. Paulina's initial introduction is followed by a sequence of instructions ('Prepare'; 'Behold') and by a number of deictics ('nothing / So aged as *this* seems'; '*thus* she stood') which, together, produce the statue as the defining spectacle of the scene and organise the characters around that central spectacle. More than this, however, Paulina is shown to be somebody who is both in control of the space of the stage and who tries hard to control how the spectacle is interpreted, including when each character might be allowed to speak:

> I like your silence; it the more shows off
> Your wonder. But yet speak; first you, my liege.

(21–22)

Perhaps this aspect of the play is already so obvious from the plot that it might seem hardly worth mentioning in relation to how the staging might work. What was interesting, however, about how we worked through the combined dialogue, gestures, and movement of the scene was the extent to which we noticed distances and proximities on stage being carefully managed. How physically close one character is able to get to another forms a constant substratum to the scene's action. And, again, it is through Paulina's words and actions that this is managed at first. When Perdita asks to kiss the hand of the statue of her mother, Paulina warns, 'O, patience! / The statue is but newly fixed; the colour's / Not dry' (46–48). She later directs the statue to 'descend' when she judges that it is time and when she has managed to capture the others in amazement. And, then, she finally allows Leontes to present his hand to the revived Hermione.

Confession: I really dislike Paulina. It is, no doubt, unprofessional to have personal animus against a character from a play, particularly a play that is more than 400 years old. And it is surely true that there are many positive things to consider about her representation in the play, especially the way that she protects Hermione from the violent misogyny and tyrannical jealousy of Leontes, the Duke and Hermione's husband. The nine-year atonement that Leontes undergoes for falsely accusing Hermione of adultery (as well as for the ensuing death of his son, Mamillius, and what he supposes to have been the murder of his baby daughter, Perdita) is something that is brought about by Paulina's care and patience. However, in the statue scene at the end of *The Winter's Tale*, where Paulina has most of her lines in the play, she behaves like one of the worst teachers you could ever imagine. Faced with a theatrical spectacle of almost impossible ambiguity (admittedly, she has set this up herself), what does she do? She tells people to sit down, to shut up, and to pay attention to her version of what they are seeing. When she does invite a response, it comes in the form of the worst kind of leading question, really telling her ~~students~~ audience what they should already be thinking:

PAULINA: Prepare
To see the life as lively mocked as ever
Still sleep mocked death. Behold and say 'tis well.

[She draws a curtain and reveals the figure of Hermione, standing like a statue]

I like your silence; it the more shows off
Your wonder. But yet speak; first you, my liege.
Comes it not something near?

(5.3.18–23)

'Behold and say 'tis well'; 'No talking at the back'; 'It might not be right but this is what the examiner will want to see.'

I assume that the 'you' of 'your silence' is a plural and refers to the assembled crowd. This becomes a singular 'you' as she zeroes in on 'my liege', the Duke himself. Leontes responds as a well-trained student and admits that the statue does indeed come more than 'something near' the lively representation of his supposedly dead wife. However, he does seem to sense that something is not quite right with what he is being both shown and told by Paulina: 'But yet, Paulina, / Hermione was not so much wrinkled, nothing / So agèd as this seems.' Just like a schoolmaster (who has not read Rancière), Paulina quickly curtails this dissenting interpretation and moves the class along until she is ready to reveal the answers.

This aspect of the scene – particularly the controlling of space, proximity, and access – is what most of my students focused on in their opening assessment of the scene. And from this initial interest, the end point of the workshop became a mapping of distances: how the different characters pull together and move apart at various moments. Approaching the scene in this way also had a particular pertinence for the direction that these workshops had started to take during the semester in reference to questions of teacherly authority. And, so, I'd like to describe a little bit about their purpose, how they came about and what were some of the results.

In 2017, I was due to teach the University of Sydney's undergraduate Shakespeare unit again. As I had done on previous occasions, one of the things that I did to prepare was to look at the lists of enrolling students to find out the kinds of degree in which they were enrolled. In a class of more than 200 students, it is one way to start thinking about the range of different kinds of experience and expectations that they are bringing with them to the course. As in previous years, there was a sizeable minority of students (roughly a third of the total enrolment) who were Bachelor of Education students. Most of these would be taking the Shakespeare course as one part of an English major within that degree and, because of this, as an aspect of their training to be high school English teachers. In that year, our faculty had made available some 'education innovation' grants, especially targeting the development of project-based learning. English is not a subject given to assessments that could be described as 'real-world projects'. However, I thought that I would see what might be done by working with this particular cohort of education students on a course within the course that focused as much on the links between the texts and what we might learn about how to teach them, as on the 'texts themselves'.[50]

With precious faculty funding in my pocket, I was able to buy out some teaching and set up a separate strand of seminars for just twenty-five of these students. They were selected at random and offered the opportunity to remove themselves from the mainstream of the Shakespeare unit, an offer that they were free to turn down. Those who took the special seminars were no longer obliged to go to their assigned tutorials although they could, if they liked, attend the lectures that were available to all. Within those separate seminars, the students undertook a number of tasks, all of which not only attempted to make sense of the plays but would also allow them to develop different teaching approaches and theories in relation to the material. Some of this was based on the outreach workshops that I had already done, as described in the sections throughout this

[50] I am grateful for the advice of two colleagues from the School of Education and Social Work – Jen Scott Curwood and Alison Grove O'Grady – for their assistance and advice on setting up the project, and to Gabriella Edelstein, who worked as a research assistant throughout the project.

Element. Some, including a workshop on *The Winter's Tale*, were freshly designed for this particular set of students. The aim was to build the students' awareness of the ways that Shakespeare's texts contain their own forms of pedagogy whilst, at the same time, giving them time to consider the ways that their knowledge of literary texts, as developed in their major, might have an impact on their future work as teachers. The 'real-world' project on which they worked was the development of some teaching plans and workshops that they would find useful in the kinds of schools in which they were doing their teaching practice. They were encouraged, where they could and if possible, to make use of these in their practical teaching experience. So far, so good. The students' experience was, according to the surveys, very good and they were pleased both with the attention being paid to their unique circumstances and with the kinds of approach that they were able to develop.

However, I am not at all sure that it worked. In fact, I don't think that it did. And, as much as I enjoyed the experience of working with these developing teachers, I have never repeated anything quite like it, even though I still maintain a particular eye on trainee teachers within the class and ensure that they know that I know that they are there, and that they can come to me with questions about Shakespeare pedagogy as well as about 'Shakespeare'. Where an impasse emerged was over the idea of the teacher as an authorising presence in the classroom. What I had foolishly not realised was the extent to which the figure of the authorising teacher was something in which this cohort of Shakespeare students/trainee teachers were profoundly invested. Of course, student-centred learning was also something that they saw as a foundational value in their emerging professional identities – and our work certainly emphasised this ethos – but it was not seen as something that they could afford to achieve at the expense of their own individual authority as teachers. Rancière's valorisation of 'ignorance' as a starting point for the teacher as well as the student was something that was anathema to their sense of themselves and of their future careers.

Where faultlines emerged in the course surveys was in occasionally expressed regrets on the part of the students that they had missed out on some of the mainstream Shakespeare unit where, they believed, they might have gained more detailed Shakespeare-specific knowledge that would afford them the capacity – the authority – to stand in front of a classroom and 'teach Shakespeare'. These were valid concerns and were, in the end, my primary reason for not repeating the experiment. However, the questions do remain for me, even as obstacles that might need to be navigated: what might disavowing explanatory authority look like in a Shakespeare classroom?

The impasse that I am thinking about here and that we discussed in these workshops is the extent to which, in the way that we have to deal pragmatically with current expectations, it is possible to step aside and allow ourselves to be 'ignorant'. For me, the question became encapsulated in what I still think of as the 'problem with Paulina'. Her requirement that we do 'awake' our belief, her control of how close people do or do not get to the statue, her predetermination of their reactions to the spectacle in which she has caught them, what these increasingly looked like in the context of this particular set of workshops was the formative artefact of contemporary education, the 'rubric'.

In high school and university teaching, predetermined course rubrics almost always inform the nature of what is learned, guiding both students and teachers towards the acknowledged aims of our teaching and learning. Students are well advised to study the requirements of the course or the exam and to ensure that their responses to the material answer to these demands. Increasingly, teachers are required to articulate how their approach to teaching will fulfil specific 'learning outcomes', as aligned with the form and content of the teaching and also with broader subject or degree-level student outcomes or, at my institution, 'graduate qualities'. The apparent transparency of this approach, whereby students find out what they can expect to learn from taking one class rather than another, should be a good thing. Or, at least, it could be a development that transfers some of the control over what is being taught and learned from the teacher to the student. This kind of scaffolded approach to teaching and learning is frequently supported with references to its nature as student-centred. Students can test the claims of what they *should* be learning against what they are being taught and, presumably, shifts in approach can be made or requested when there appears to be a mismatch between the two. A potential problem of these approaches, however, is that it is not always possible to determine, in advance, what might be learned from studying something. If we already knew what we were going to learn when we start to read, then we would likely already have read the book. Macbeth had it right when he said that '[i]f the assessment could trammel up the consequence and catch with its surcease, success then "learning outcomes" would always make sense'. Or something like that.

To assume the ends of learning from its beginnings does not necessarily afford students the level of control over the experience that is sometimes claimed; rather it can be a means to curtail the experience of learning through producing them as compliant subjects, tied to specific modes of thought. If the authority of the teacher is somewhat diminished by outsourcing the aims and objectives of teaching to what often turn out to be pre-packaged, stock 'outcomes', that authority is not transferred to the student so much as to what then becomes the necessarily anonymous institution of the secondary or tertiary education organisation. The requirements of the new learning rubric are often written in the passive mode that, elsewhere, we are taught not to use: 'It is required that'. Or, rather, the passive mode silently underpins the grammar of the rubrics which is only speciously active. Even when they are written as 'Students will be able to', the ends are confidently assumed before a single book has been picked up. Use of 'will' in these rubrics purports to afford students some agency in their own learning whilst simultaneously removing it. Paulina would, I think, have been very much at home in the world of rubrics and learning outcomes. 'It is required that you do awake your beliefs': like all good rubrics this obfuscates agency (required by who or what?) whilst, at the same time, controlling both the knowledge contained within the spectacle and how it can legitimately be interpreted if you are to pass her test.

Paulina's control of the scene, however, is reversed by the time that we get to the end of the scene. Once the reconciliations have been brought about, it is Leontes whose dialogue contains the same combination of instructions (for the characters) and stage directions (for the actors):

Good Paulina,
Lead us from hence, where we may leisurely
Each one demand and answer to his part
Performed in this wide gap of time since first
We were dissevered. Hastily lead away.

(152–56)

Despite Paulina having done all the work up until this point, Leontes appears to swoop in at the last minute and take charge of the play's happy endings, enjoining everybody 'hastily' to leave the stage and Paulina's gallery. In parsing the scene's games with proximity and distance, this last transfer of authority is something that the students in the *Winter's Tale* seminar particularly noted, prompting amongst us two discussions: one about the difficult and disappointing gender dynamics of the play, and the other about the equally difficult dynamics of our own classroom.

The transfer of authority at the end of *The Winter's Tale* – from Paulina to Leontes – is the stuff of comedy, and of tragicomedy, conflict resolved in a restoration of order. Here, it is the patriarchal order that earlier revealed itself as open to deep corruption, now in its restoration apparently schooled away from its violent excesses. But does theatre and/or education always have to be so transactional, the passing on of the baton of knowledge and authority from one person to another, one set of people to another? Anonymous feedback on this education-oriented stream of the Shakespeare unit considered those questions. Where one student enjoyed the way that it 'encouraged ownership of the texts', another (possibly even the same student?) worried that 'Students were given too much agency'. Where one student was keen on the way that the workshops 'showed me new ways of teaching Shakespeare, beyond just teaching them around a central theme of the play', another criticised the way that the unit seemingly ignored the practicalities of high school teaching: 'In my opinion quality university teaching looks and acts differently to quality school teaching; on occasion some awkward moments in the course came as a result of some of these different perspectives.'

What these responses skirt around is something that we discussed more directly in class: who was in charge of knowing things about Shakespeare? At times, it was clear that the students felt that I was short-changing them by holding back, withholding my own expertise in favour of providing platforms for them to develop their own reading strategies. They, I think, wanted to be Leontes to my Paulina. This impasse – and our discomfort with the ending of *The Winter's Tale* – asks questions about whether it is ever possible to disavow authority. The answer seems to be that it isn't. Where the distribution of knowledge is at play, questions of authority emerge: who knows what? who remains ignorant (genuinely or otherwise)? what strategies are used to produce either ignorance or revelation in a student? As much as Paulina and our contemporary rubrics ('it is required') offer to generalise the imperative to gain certain kinds of knowledge in certain kinds of way, obfuscating the authorising context within which this is to take place, the question or problem of authority never really leaves us when dealing with teaching or with drama.

The structures of drama – comedy, tragicomedy, and tragedy – seem necessarily to trade in uneven distributions of knowledge. Likewise, the means by which Shakespeare's own players put on their shows involved a peculiar distribution of ignorance and knowledge, with individual actors knowing little about the production other than their own lines. What I have hoped to argue and to show in this Element, however, is that there are elements of 'Shakespeare' – the way that its dialogue demands, at times, a certain kind of simple action-oriented reading and the way that its scenes are structured around dramatic irony – which afford ways into the plays that don't always aggregate knowledge to the teacher. There is nothing pure about these methods. Teachers have authority and always will have because of their position within the authorising institutions for which they work (such as schools, universities, education authorities, and exam boards), but this need not always lend itself to the production of what Rancière identifies as the damage of explicatory teaching, a form of teaching that produces deficit even as it claims to eradicate it. If we can't eliminate the sense that education is always, somehow, engaged in a 'work of grieving', we can occasionally glimpse other possibilities.

Conclusion: 'Treasons make me wish myself a beggar'

I started with Richard on the battlements of Flint Castle, and with the actor learning that he didn't need to know everything to start making sense of his performance and of Richard's predicament. At the close of the play, Richard is murdered in prison. Beforehand, he is alone in his cell. Left to his own devices, he dreams up a world in which he plays at being everybody:

> I have been studying how I may compare
> This prison where I live unto the world;
> And for because the world is populous,
> And here is not a creature but myself,
> I cannot do it. Yet I'll hammer it out.
> My brain I'll prove the female to my soul,
> My soul the father, and these two beget
> A generation of still-breeding thoughts;
> And these same thoughts people this little world
> In humours like the people of this world,
> For no thought is contented.
>
> (5.5.1–11)

He dreams up a world of contention and difference, the only world that he has known and the only world that we know, both from dramatic fiction and the classroom. The multitudes that Richard dreams up, he reduces to two options, a beggar or a king:

> Sometimes am I king;
> Then treasons make me wish myself a beggar,
> And so I am. Then crushing penury
> Persuades me I was better when a king;
> Then am I kinged again, and by and by,
> Think that I am unkinged by Bolingbroke,
> And straight am nothing.
>
> (32–48)

The only escape from the endless transfer of power that Richard seems trapped within and that has also been the defining narrative of his life – of the life of the country – is his death, is becoming 'nothing'. No man, he says, will be 'pleased till he be eased / With being nothing'. This final abdication brings an end to the questions or problems of authority with which the play has been concerned, at least for Richard. Stay silent. Exit stage left.

The world in which we live and breathe, either as educators or as Shakespeareans, is one that is defined by the question, or problem, of authority. To dream of an end to authority is to dream of an end to the world that we inhabit, and that we bring into being the moment that we enter a classroom and start to 'hammer it out'. But it is still possible to teach with the troublesome idea that the real pleasure might, after all, lie in giving up (if only for a few moments) our teacherly claims to make sense of the world.

Bibliography

Akhimie, Patricia. 'Cultivating Expertise: Glossing Shakespeare and Race', *Literature Compass* 18.10 (2021), pp. 1–8. https://doi.org/10.1111/lic3.12607.

Astington, John. *Actors and Acting in Shakespeare's Time: The Art of Stage Playing* (Cambridge: Cambridge University Press, 2010).

Australian Government, *Review of Higher Education Final Report* (Canberra: Commonwealth of Australia, 2008).

Bates, Catherine. 'Teaching Queer Theory: Judith Butler, Queer Theory, and *She's the Man*', in Alice Ferrebe and Fiona Tolan (Eds.), *Teaching Gender* (London: Palgrave, 2012), pp. 47–62.

Belsey, Catherine. 'Shakespeare's Sad Tale for Winter: *Hamlet* and the Tradition of Fireside Ghost Stories', *Shakespeare Quarterly* 61.1 (2010), pp. 1–27. https://doi.org/100.1353/shq.0.0136.

Bodin, Jean. *On Sovereignty: Four Chapters from the Six Books of the Commonwealth*, Ed. Julian H. Franklin (Cambridge: Cambridge University Press, 1997).

Booth, Wayne C. *A Rhetoric of Irony* (Chicago: The University of Chicago Press, 1974).

Brown, David Sterling. '(Early) Modern Literature: Crossing the Color Line', *Radical Teacher* 105 (2016), pp. 69–77. https://doi.org/10.5195/rt.2016.255.

Chalmers, Jim and Clare, Jason. '20,000 New University Places to Target Skills Shortages' (media release; 17 August 2022) https://ministers.education.gov.au/chalmers/20000-new-university-places-target-skill-shortages.

Christofides, Roger M. 'Hamlet versus Othello: Or, Why the White Boy Keeps Winning', *Shakespeare* 17.1 (2021), pp. 6–14. https://doi.org/10.1080/17450918.2020.1829020.

Cohen, Ralph. 'Original Staging and the Shakespeare Classroom', in Millia Riggio (Ed.), *Teaching Shakespeare through Performance* (New York: Modern Language Society of America, 1999). pp. 78–101.

Dadabhoy, Ambereen. 'Skin in the Game: Teaching Race in Early Modern Literature', *Studies in Medieval and Renaissance Teaching* 27.2 (2020), pp. 97–111.

Eaglestone, Robert. *Literature: Why It Matters* (Cambridge, MA: Polity, 2019).

Eskew, Doug. 'Shakespeare, Alienation, and the Working-Class Student', in Sharon O'Dair and Timothy Francisco (Eds.), *Shakespeare and the 99%: Literary Studies, the Profession, and the Production of Inequity* (London: Palgrave, 2019), pp. 37–56.

Evans, Arthur C. 'Friendship in *Hamlet*', *Comparative Drama* 33.1 (1999), pp. 88–124.

Forker, Charles R. 'Introduction', in William Shakespeare (Ed.), *King Richard II* (London: Arden Shakespeare, 2002). pp.1–64.

McCarthy, Harry. '"M[aster] Monkesters Schollars: Richard Mulcaster, Physical Education, and the Early Modern Boy Companies', *Early Theatre* 24.2 (2021), pp. 31–54. https://doi.org/10.12745/et.24.2.4390.

McManus, Clare. '"Sing It Like Poor Barbary": *Othello* and Early Modern Women's Performance', *Shakespeare Bulletin* 33.1 (2015), pp. 99–120. https://doi.org/0.1353/shb.2015.0013.

Neill, Michael. *Issues of Death: Mortality and Identity in English Renaissance Tragedy* (Oxford: Oxford University Press, 1997).

Palfrey, Simon. *Shakespeare's Possible Worlds* (Cambridge: Cambridge University Press, 2014).

Palfrey, Simon and Stern, Tiffany. *Shakespeare in Parts* (Oxford: Oxford University Press, 2007).

Rancière, Jacques. *The Ignorant Schoolmaster: Five Lessons in Intellectual Emancipation*, Tr. K. Ross (Stanford: Stanford University Press, 1991).

Sedgewick, Garnett G. *Of Irony, Especially in Drama* (Toronto: University of Toronto Press, 1948).

Semler, Liam. *Teaching Shakespeare and Marlowe: Learning versus the System* (London: Bloomsbury, 2013).

Shakespeare, William. *The New Oxford Shakespeare*, Eds. Terri Bourus, Gabriel Egan, John Jowett, and Gary Taylor (Oxford: Oxford University Press, 2016).

Shannon, Laurie. *Sovereign Amity: Figures of Friendship in Shakespearean Contexts* (Chicago: The University of Chicago Press, 2002).

Sinfield, Alan. 'How to Read *The Merchant of Venice* without Being Heterosexist', in T. Hawkes (Ed.), *Alternative Shakespeares 2* (London: Routledge, 1996), pp. 135–52.

Stern, Tiffany. *Making Shakespeare: From Stage to Page* (London: Routledge, 2004).

Syme, Holger. 'The Theater of Shakespeare's Time', in *The Norton Shakespeare* (3rd ed.), Ed. S. Greenblatt (New York: Norton, 2015), pp. 93–118.

Thompson, Ayanna and Turchi, Laura. *Teaching Shakespeare with Purpose: A Student-Centred Approach* (London: Bloomsbury, 2016).

Thomson, Leslie. *From Playtext to Performance on the Early Modern Stage: How Did They Do It?* (London: Routledge, 2022).

Tillyard, Eustace M. W. *The Elizabethan World Picture* (London: Macmillan 1942).

Tribble, Evelyn. *Cognition in the Globe: Attention and Memory in Shakespeare's Theatre* (New York: Palgrave, 2011).

Early Modern Actors and Shakespeare's Theatre: Thinking with the Body (London: Bloomsbury, 2017).

TSFX (The School for Excellence), 'How Does Shakespeare Use Imagery to Portray Challenging Ideas about Truth and Deceit in *Hamlet*?' www.tsfx .edu.au/resources/how-does-shakespeare-use-imagery-to-portray-chal lenging-ideas-about-truth-and-deceit-in-hamlet/.

Traub, Valerie. *Desire and Anxiety: Circulations of Sexuality in Shakespearean Drama* (London: Routledge, 1992).

West, Caitlin. 'Implied Stage Directions in Shakespeare: A Workshop Approach', *Metaphor* 2 (2021), pp. 24–28. https://doi.org/10.3316/informit.728623726241444.

Acknowlegements

I would like to thank the students and colleagues who have participated in the various workshops that have helped the development of ideas contained in this Element. Students include those from Bankstown Girls High School, Blacktown Boys High School, Holroyd School, Willyama High School in Broken Hill, and the University of Sydney. The support of their teachers has also been both illuminating and very welcome. Colleagues from the University of Sydney with whom I worked on our 'LINK' project include Melissa Hardie, Annamarie Jagose, Peter Kirkpatrick, Kate Lilley, Peter Marks, Kieryn McKay, Nicola Parsons, Brigid Rooney, and Beth Yahp. Gabriella Edelstein worked with me as a teaching assistant on the workshops with Bachelor of Education students, contributing her considerable knowledge, skill, and attention to detail. Other colleagues have also worked on the outreach project over time and an unexpected outcome of the project has been a marked change in the culture of the English department over these years, becoming more collegiate and welcoming as it turned its face more fully towards the outside world. I would also like to thank the series editors, Liam Semler and Gillian Woods, for both the opportunity and their patience. My Sydney colleague, Liam, has long been a guiding light in the pursuit of ethical and generative pedagogies.

Shakespeare and Pedagogy

Liam E. Semler
The University of Sydney

Liam E. Semler is Professor of Early Modern Literature in the Department of English at the University of Sydney. He is author of *Teaching Shakespeare and Marlowe: Learning versus the System* (2013) and co-editor (with Kate Flaherty and Penny Gay) of *Teaching Shakespeare beyond the Centre: Australasian Perspectives* (2013). He is editor of *Coriolanus: A Critical Reader* (2021) and co-editor (with Claire Hansen and Jackie Manuel) of *Reimagining Shakespeare Education: Teaching and Learning through Collaboration* (Cambridge, 2023). His most recent book outside Shakespeare studies is *The Early Modern Grotesque: English Sources and Documents 1500–1700* (2019). Liam leads the Better Strangers project which hosts the open-access Shakespeare Reloaded website (shakespearereloaded.edu.au).

Gillian Woods
Birkbeck College, University of London

Gillian Woods is Reader in Renaissance Literature and Theatre at Birkbeck College, University of London. She is the author of *Shakespeare's Unreformed Fictions* (2013; joint winner of Shakespeare's Globe Book Award), *Romeo and Juliet: A Reader's Guide to Essential Criticism* (2012), and numerous articles about Renaissance drama. She is the co-editor (with Sarah Dustagheer) of *Stage Directions and Shakespearean Theatre* (2018). She is currently working on a new edition of

A Midsummer Night's Dream for Cambridge University Press, as well as a Leverhulme-funded monograph about Renaissance Theatricalities. As founding director of the Shakespeare Teachers' Conversations, she runs a seminar series that brings together university academics, school teachers and educationalists from non-traditional sectors, and she regularly runs workshops for schools.

ABOUT THE SERIES

The teaching and learning of Shakespeare around the world is complex and changing. Elements in Shakespeare and Pedagogy synthesises theory and practice, including provocative, original pieces of research, as well as dynamic, practical engagements with learning contexts.

Cambridge Elements ☰

Shakespeare and Pedagogy

Printed in the United States
by Baker & Taylor Publisher Services